RETIREMENT PLANNING AT 40 AND BEYOND

SIMPLE GUIDE TO TAKE CONTROL OF YOUR FUTURE,
YOUR FINANCES, YOUR INVESTMENTS, AND TIME IN
RETIREMENT TO THE NEXT LEVEL IN 30 DAYS

RICHARD HOLT

CONTENTS

INTRODUCTION

Don't simply retire from something; have something to retire to.

— HARRY EMERSON FOSDICK

Scout. Stash. Use. Repeat. That is how an average squirrel behaves when foraging for food. I know this seems quite out-of-place in a book on financial planning, but if you pay close attention, you might find that this behavior is surprisingly relevant to planning for retirement. Squirrels might have cracked the code that we humans often find difficult to grasp. Whether it's their "scatter-hoarding" whereby they bury their nuts in several places rather than in one stash, or their agile tendency to aptly use their stash during the winters, our rodent friends seem to have quite the retirement lessons for us.

No matter how much we pretend that mere financial planning and number-crunching is going to get us through our retirement, the truth remains that retirement, all said and done, is an intimate affair. It means a different thing to each one of us, and that vision dramatically impacts how we approach retirement planning as a whole. For one individual, retirement may be the beginning of the second act where they nurture their passions rather than obligations; it might be opening up a restaurant to satisfy their desire to be a chef. For another, it might be sunbathing on a beach in Bali with their partner. For someone else, it might be the beginning of a new career altogether. The point is that retirement is as personal as your career aspirations have been thus far and must be treated as such.

Regardless of how diverse everyone's plans may be in the context of retirement, one thing is for sure—it's going to require substantial financial stability to get there. And it is the journey that you will make from here to that point that will make all the difference to your peace of mind. The fact that you have picked up this book indeed tells me that you are ready to make that journey. But even having decided to walk the path to managing your financial resources, there might still be a considerable number of obstacles in the way.

Having worked in the financial sector for years, I find that people are often perplexed about the way forward. You would expect that with the information boom facilitated by the internet, people's confusion would be reduced. In my experience, I have found that the exact opposite is true. There's so much information available on so many routes to the ever-elusive financial stability that people are most often driven into analysis paralysis, ultimately keeping them stuck in ineffective financial patterns. And even those that decide to go ahead with the advice they have found online tend to rely a little too much on the authenticity of the internet to guide them in their financial journeys. Following unreliable financial advice can be disastrously harmful, sometimes even worse than doing nothing about their dysfunctional financial situation.

WHY THIS BOOK?

I do not claim that this book will put all your retirement worries to rest straight away; indeed, no one can make that claim. Remember that your retirement is all about you and your priorities, which cannot be contained in one book. I strongly urge you to take professional financial advice before you make any significant decisions in this regard. Your life dynamics need to be reflected in your financial choices as well, after all. But there are some tips and tricks which, if you follow them, can put you on the best path to hit a bull's eye in your financial management.

Having worked in finance, I have experienced many people who have come to me for financial advice, both in my professional as well as personal capacity. For a long time now, I have made it my topmost priority to take the time to understand people's actual retirement needs thoroughly before giving out any "pearls of financial wisdom," as one of my friends calls them jokingly. But as invested as I have been in the financial sector all my adult life, and as many people as I may have guided through their financial journeys, there were still things that I struggled with when taking up the task of retirement planning. It was then that I realized that if I, being from the financial sector, could find this phase challenging, a person with no financial background could easily get overwhelmed.

I am writing this book with the sole aim of reaching out to those that feel that retirement finances are simply out of their grasp. I will outline my own challenges and those of my clients that we have encountered over the years, and I will attempt to help you draw out a concrete plan.

Most people tend to keep a fair distance from dealing with their finances because they believe it's all about boring number-crunching, dull budgets, drab schemes, and, overall, just about everything that's "too complicated." Let me tell you, though retirement in itself is a complicated construct, planning for it doesn't have to be. If done in a disciplined and organized manner, it can simplify a great many aspects of your life. However, too many people get caught up in outdated ideas about retirement planning and complicate their lives by applying old concepts to their current modern-day circumstances.

Remember that retirement isn't the same as it was only ten years ago. A lot has changed and continues to change. It's paramount that these changes are taken into account when planning for the next phase of your life. As much as I'd like it to be about actual financial numbers, retirement is also a life stage that's accompanied by significant changes, both physical and emotional. Anyone who tells you that retirement planning is just a numbers game is kidding themselves.

My purpose in writing this book is to provide a unique perspective on these changes as well as the financial measures that you can take to cope with them. The idea is to simplify the latest relevant financial concepts in a way that you can incorporate them seamlessly into your life.

OVERVIEW OF THE BOOK

In order to utilize this book in the best way possible, it would be beneficial to understand what this book is and what it is not. This book does not give you a detailed perspective on growing your investments. Though we talk about all the essential points in retirement planning in fine detail, tackling each of the financial instruments in elaborate detail falls outside the purview of this book. This book is meant to be a financial guide that decodes financial technicalities and jargon for the novice.

I strongly recommend that you first do a quick run-through of the chapters presented here, just reading through them once. Then go back and read it again with the exclusive aim of formulating your particular financial plan and begin to put the first steps into motion. This way, you can absorb the content in its entirety before thinking about how it applies to your personal circumstances. You can also make use of the checklists at the end of some chapters to help you keep pace with the details discussed in the book.

Through this book, I attempt to tackle the issues related to retirement planning in an increasing order of complexity. Chapter One: *Retiring On Your Own Terms* sets the foundation to help put you into the right state of mind for the coming chapters. This chapter tackles the widely-talked-about budgeting process and gives a stepwise procedure to incorporate it into your life. In this chapter, we also talk about the basic principles that ensure that our retirement planning stays on track.

Chapter Two: *Health Is Wealth* is about a topic that not all financial experts talk about, and yet it's one of the most crucial. In this chapter, we attempt to dig into the concept of all-around health and its implications for your wealth planning.

Chapter Three: *Of Savings and Investments* deals with core financial understanding by highlighting effective retirement savings options as well as investment avenues to grow your wealth. The options discussed are all-encompassing, so you can pick and choose the ones that apply best to you.

In Chapter Four: *Optimizing Your Portfolio,* we take a deep dive into the ways through which you can maximize your returns per your risk tolerance. We also discuss the idea of generating more income in order to boost your savings rate.

Chapter Five: *Prepping for the Big Day* takes you a step further in your retirement planning by exploring ideas to prepare financially as well as mentally to embrace the approaching new phase of your life. This highlights some of the tough sentimental choices you might need to make, as well as some of the legal tasks that you will have to complete in order to ensure that things keep running smoothly after you pass away.

Chapter Six: *Spending the Big Bucks* takes us into the economic aspects that might hinder your retirement life and also talks about the various withdrawal strategies that you might find helpful.

In Chapter Seven: *Hacking Retirement,* I address the most frequently asked questions, highlight the most commonly made mistakes and reveal the golden rules that successful retirees never miss out on. With the theoretical knowledge backing your understanding at this point, these tips and tricks are designed to have a more practical outlook.

And last comes Chapter Eight: *The Perfect Retirement,* which is designed to help you enjoy your retirement as best as you can. This chapter aims to help you look beyond the financial side of retirement planning and address it as both an experience of vulnerability and an opportunity for tremendous growth. Only when you view it in its entirety will you be able to truly appreciate the importance of retirement planning and move ahead with purpose.

As you will note, this book mainly highlights the schemes, policies, and technicalities within the American system. Though the names might be different, other countries will have similar, if not the same, schemes. If you do not reside in the U.S., then I urge you to discover the equivalent of these schemes, policies, etc., in your own country. When creating a plan, if you are unsure, seek reliable financial advice; remember, the internet is not always a reliable source, and random sources should not be used to make crucial financial decisions.

You are now on the path to financial success, and even though it may seem foggy at present, as you move through these chapters, you'll see the fog lift. The important thing is that you take the first step, and with deliberation and initiative, the rest will fall into place. So, step in; your perfect retirement plan awaits!

RETIRING ON YOUR OWN TERMS

The question isn't at what age I want to retire; it's at what income.

— GEORGE FOREMAN

There's one thing that inevitably happens to me at parties—people come up to me and strike up casual conversations about finance. Well... finance because they know I'm good at it, and casual because they think I'll just give some superficial generic advice that they might benefit from. Here's what most of them don't know about me. To me, there's nothing casual about finances. So, typically, I end up asking them questions about their life situation, and one aspect that comes up invariably in one form or another is retirement. It's almost funny how the word 'retirement' immediately and simultaneously brings out a wishful and a fearful expression on people's faces.

If there's one thing I have learned from working with people and their finances, it is that fear doesn't blend well with financial choices. And that fear is the direct result of one particular question, which is enough to scare the living daylights out of anyone: Am I doing enough? This one question has the potential to open Pandora's box and unravel any desire to work on finances at all. Am I doing the right thing? What if my plans don't pan out the way I want them to? Am I saving enough? The questions are endless. And the harsh reality is that no matter how neat your financial plans are, life has a way of throwing us curveballs way more often than we expect. Ultimately, 20/20 vision is only possible in retrospect.

So, rather than experiencing anxiety over the future, I urge my clients to keep it simple in the present, pay attention to the tiny things that they can do, and, most importantly, enjoy the finances that they have all worked so hard to achieve. Through this book, I wish to change the traditional attitude towards financial management as a compulsion springing from a fear of the future and encourage you to play around with your money in a way that allows you to derive pleasure from it now as well as in the future.

THE BURDEN OF BUDGETING

Someone said the other day that, considering that retirement gives you the freedom to do anything you desire, there should be a better, more adventurous, and exciting name for it. But the unfortunate reality is that not everyone thinks of this as a positive thing. Many people get too tangled up in "what ought to be" in retirement without much consideration for their own needs and personal circumstances. Remember, your retirement is all about you. And who knows you better than you?! That is why you are the only one who can plan your retirement. The best way to do this is to toss away your apprehensions about the future and embrace your visualization of the future that brings you true joy.

More than a statistical figure, retirement planning is about making sure that you still have a steady flow of income coming in, even when you are not actively earning it. This used to be a much simpler process a few decades ago when one would routinely work the same job for three to four decades. Then when the time came, one would bid farewell to one's responsibilities at the workplace and switch to a leisure mode filled with employer-funded pension plans.

This is no longer the case. Now, before you start panicking, hear me out—while the current departure from these traditional retirement plans may seem like a situation warranting anxiety, it also means that now, rather than your employer, *you* are the one at the helm of your retirement planning. Once you embrace this fact, the opportunities are virtually infinite.

A Simple Budgeting Strategy

As I said before, most people tend to shy away from financial planning because they expect it to be over-whelmingly complicated. But as you will discover throughout this book, though the process is detailed, it certainly doesn't need to be complicated. One of the most 'complicated' tasks of financial planning is the creation of an effective budget. And people almost invariably hate the task of budgeting. In my decades' worth of experience, I have yet to find someone who loves the idea of budgeting straight off the bat. And the reason for this aversion is quite apparent too—budgets are, after all, meant to be tools to restrict our financial spending, aren't they? Aren't they supposed to be dull and boring, with no room for fun at all? Do these thoughts seem like they are straight from your head? Well, if you said yes, you are not the only one. But what if I answered both those questions about budgets in the negative? What if I told you that budgets aren't supposed to restrict but make your financial spending more efficient? That they are not dull but can be quite fun to create, at least once you get used to them.

Creating an effective budget is something we just cannot bypass on our retirement-planning journeys. You may decide to call it financial planning if the 'B-word is too overwhelming for you. So, we might as well get comfortable with that idea. I often urge my clients to start with the most straightforward strategy there is —the 50/30/20 rule. Whether you are looking to save for retirement or just come up with an effective budget, this is a rule of thumb you should definitely familiarize yourself with. This rule was initially popularized by Elizabeth Warren in her book *All Your Worth: The Ultimate Lifetime Money Plan* (2006). The idea is simple— divide your income after taxes into three basic categories of needs, wants, and savings, allocating 50%, 30%, and 20% respectively to each category.

As you may have guessed from these aptly named categories, the needs are the payments that you absolutely need to make to survive, like electricity, groceries, rent, etc. You cannot waive these off no matter what. Wants are essential things that you can live without. As fun and relaxing as it is to go to the movies or out for dinner once in a while, it's still not essential for survival. People seem to lose their way the most in this particular category. They either splurge on things way beyond their budgets or cut this spending out entirely in an attempt to devise a perfect budget. Neither is helpful because, without making space for an appropriate amount of leisure, we run the risk of losing perspective and falling through the cracks way more. And the last category is the one we tend to ignore most often—savings. Allocating a meager 20% of your monthly income can boost your savings by a significant amount.

This rule may seem a little too simple to be effective, but several of my clients have benefited from this numeric allocation of resources, and so can you! I'd say it's the simplicity that makes it so very easy to implement. All you really have to do is divide your income into these three categories at the beginning of each month. This can be done with either physical cash or with your digital money. Most people find it extremely useful to use the envelope system to implement this budgeting technique.

In the envelope system, you'd essentially calculate 50%, 30%, and 20% of your paycheck (after taxes) and keep each of these amounts in separate envelopes. Once the amounts are placed in each envelope, though, there is no going back. So, if you run out of your 'wants' money and you still really want to go out with your friends, you cannot dip into your savings envelope, even if it's with a promise to replace the money as soon as possible. I particularly like the envelope system because it makes the 50/30/20 rule of budgeting tangible and thus more real. This is undoubtedly helpful when establishing the discipline to stick to this budget.

If you are someone who keeps their funds in a digital form, there is no need to worry either. There are multiple online apps like Goodbudget, Mvelopes, SimpleBudget, etc. that use a virtual envelope system to help you track your budget. I recommend that you give the free version a try and then go for a paid version of the app most suited to you.

Emergency Fund: Yay or Nay?

You'd often find that discussions surrounding budgets emphasize the maintenance of an emergency fund. They tell you that a budget without an emergency fund is bound to shatter the moment a financial crisis arrives. Though this may seem like prudent advice, I find that an overly cautious approach towards your finances can do you more harm than good. I know this is a pretty unconventional thing to express in a financial planning book, but hear me out.

Many experts will urge you to build three, six, or eight months' worth of your paycheck into an inert fund to help you through potential emergencies. While there is merit to the idea of having a tiny money box to dip into in times of disaster, you should also be aware that this money box will lie there, completely useless for the most of your life. These funds could easily be redirected into a much more productive avenue. Remember that even though it may feel like it, we don't live in as volatile a time as we used to. Now, I do not deny that we are more vulnerable in terms of job security; yes, layoffs are an unfortunate reality that we have to live with. But, and this is a big but, the question is: are emergency funds the only (or even the most efficient) way to stave off these uncertainties?

The answer is: not always. What I have come to find through my experience is that anyone who can afford to set aside a big chunk of their paycheck for an emergency fund usually belongs to a class of employees that has considerable employment benefits. One of these benefits, for instance, is unemployment insurance, which you can utilize in the case of a layoff crisis. Obviously, this does not make for an ideal situation, but one wouldn't be any better off with their emergency fund than they would be with unemployment insurance.

Now, no matter what I say, life has a way of surprising us every now and then, or rather, should I say, especially when we least expect it? Have you ever been in a situation when you felt like you finally had a grip on your life, and just then, your car broke down? Yes, of course, you have; we all have. And it's these situations that financial experts use as their core advocacy concerns in favor of emergency funds. And, sure, it seems reasonable enough to have just enough cash on you to cover such unexpected expenses. I generally tell my clients to keep aside about $1,000 for themselves. It's the money that's tied into funds beyond these expenses that life throws at you that can restrict your financial movement considerably.

And to think of it, would you really call these 'emergencies' or just something that happens in life every once in a while? I have found that most of my clients believe that it's the latter. An emergency, for most people, means a situation that can seriously threaten their well-being. And sorry to burst the emergency fund bubble, but a truly serious emergency can rarely be covered with a typical emergency fund, surely not for too long!

Another reason I advise almost all my clients against these emergency funds is that since they need to be accessible, they have to be kept in liquid form in a savings account. If you are even slightly familiar with banking policies, you will know that savings accounts give pretty bad returns in terms of interest rates. These interest rates likely don't even keep pace with inflation. So, if you think about it, you are actually losing money as it lies dormant in an emergency fund in your bank. The wiser thing to do would be to assess your own unique situation rather than practice the financial cliches of days gone by and make a decision regarding how you'd want to utilize your funds to the best possible extent. The idea is not to engage in reckless risk-taking but to assess the risk as best as possible to ensure that you aren't losing out on growth opportunities.

THE BUDGET BREAKDOWN, RETIREMENT STYLE

Now that we have addressed the budget elephant in the room, it's time to ease into the specific niche of planning a retirement budget. The basics of budget planning, of course, remain the same, but when planning for retirement specifically, there are a few more aspects we need to consider. Before we get into that exercise, though, it's important to remember that your budget, in addition to giving you a financial roadmap, will also be the practice ground for inculcating the financial discipline that you need to not just survive retirement but flourish and grow through it. With that in mind, utilizing budgets as a tool to plan for retirement rather than financial planning during retirement is quite beneficial. So, let's get started with the stepwise approach to planning a retirement budget.

Step 1: Calculating the Amount of Money Required After Retirement

So, how do you plan for an event that's, maybe, one or two decades into the future? Though the actual figure may vary widely depending on the individual, most financial experts agree that if you wish to maintain a comfortable lifestyle even after leaving the workforce, your annual retirement income should be roughly 80% of the annual income you make before you retire. However, this figure cannot be taken as written in stone, as factors like pensions, social security, part-time jobs, health expenses, and even the standard of living that you desire will impact this figure positively or negatively.

As you might have guessed, the scope of this step is quite broad in that the aspects of your life that may require you to spend money after retirement may be virtually endless. Thus, let's break it down and look at specific main categories of expenses.

- healthcare
- rent/mortgage
- debt
- taxes
- food expenses
- commute
- leisure
- wardrobe

Note that all of the above areas of expenditure are already a part of your current budget. But be careful not to use those numbers straight from your last month's budget. You need to take the data of at least the last year to estimate the general trend that your expenses are moving in. Remember, the more data you have to make this analysis, the more accurate it's likely to be. And that's why, if you haven't started with budgeting yet, it's high time you do, if not for your present money management, then at least for the sake of your future financial planning.

Step 2: Calculating the Money You Will Make After Retirement

Retirement isn't simply about spending all that you have earned. Much to the contrary, it's about ensuring there is a steady stream of income, even though it may not be as big as your working income. The idea behind financial planning is that when it's time for you to retire, you already have multiple sources through which money is trickling in.

1. Social Security: Social Security may make up a significant chunk of a retiree's income. Depending on when this is applied for, the benefits may be slightly different, but on average, they range roughly around 40% of your pre-retirement income. Though on the face of it, this may seem simple enough, there are a couple of crucial decisions you'll need to make to reap the most significant number of benefits:

    a) The age at which you retire
    b) Whether or not you claim the spousal benefits

For example, while most people have their full retirement age (FRA) at 66, they do not know that they can earn more benefits if they start to claim benefits at 70. Also, if both spouses are of retirement age, you might do better to claim the spousal benefits and let yours grow in the meantime. Then, when you turn 70, you can claim your higher benefits, thereby gaining a considerably more significant sum.

2. Defined benefit plans: These are synonymous with pension plans and include the retirement plans that are sponsored by your employer. The calculations for these are set out in specific formulas. Thus both parties—the employers and the employees—have the advantage of knowing in advance exactly how much the employee will be receiving post-retirement, facilitating future planning. Another advantage to the employees is that the employer bears the planning and investment risks and can be legally held liable if they go back on what was agreed initially.

Like social security, the number of defined benefit plans can also vary according to the age of retirement and, consequently, the number of years you have worked at the job. For instance, working an extra year may lead to more significant pension benefits by increasing the number of years of service factor in the calculation formula or simply by fetching you an increased income in that extra year, thus boosting your final salary figure.

The payout of such benefit plans may happen in one of several ways:

a) a single-life annuity that pays the employee a fixed amount every month until death
b) a qualified joint and survivor annuity which pays the fixed monthly amount until death and then can be collected by the surviving spouse

c) or lastly, a lump-sum payout, which pays the employee the whole amount in one single go

3. Defined contribution plans: These are tax-deferred plans that allow investment earnings to accumulate tax-free until a constructive receipt of the profits is received. This means that the employee contributes a fixed portion of his paycheck to a fund that keeps accumulating. In some cases, the employer too may match the employee's contribution, leading to a considerable chunk to be harvested after retirement. 401 (k) and 403 (b) are the most common schemes in this category and are certainly ones that demand your attention.

Individual Retirement Accounts (IRAs) are set up independently by the employee without the help of the employer. We'll differentiate between Roth and traditional IRAs in a later chapter, where we'll look at all of these instruments in much greater detail. For now, it's essential that you understand the importance of these plans and their contribution to your retirement income as a whole.

4. Savings: This, as I said before, is the most contentious aspect among retirement planners as it's the most relevant to them in real-time. This is eventually about the money that you have stashed up in your bank accounts.

5. Investments and passive income: These are the financial elements that will give you the most significant returns. An investment in stocks and mutual funds, for instance, can help your money grow exponentially. Also, creating sources of passive income like property rent is a brilliant idea because after retirement, rather than working for your money, making your money work for you is a much smarter approach to take.

6. Part-time employment: Though employment opportunities for retirees are quite restricted, you might decide to try your luck still. This may include starting a new side hustle and maybe something you have always wanted to do. Of course, you can't know now if you will be employed at 60+, but the point is to make your best estimate about whether you want to or not.

Now, this is not where this step ends—rather, the contrary. There's a lot of debate over how much money you need to save for retirement. One rule that used to be agreed upon by most is the 4% rule. This rule essentially states that if you withdraw around 4% of your retirement savings in the first year and then adjust the withdrawals for inflation, your retirement savings can last you a comfortable 30 years at least.

To calculate your estimate of the retirement amount required, add the retirement balances from your retirement accounts because of the apparent reason that you can only be certain of these accounts, let's say your traditional and Roth IRA. (The amount from all the other sources would vary depending on years of service, pre-retirement income, etc.) Let's say these IRA accounts add up to a total of $500,000. Take this amount as it is if you plan to retire soon; if not, you might want to consider the expected growth that will accrue to this amount. Multiply this amount by 4%, which gives you $20,000. This would be your 4%. So, go ahead and divide your 4% by 12 months, which would give you roughly $1667. This means that you can withdraw around that amount every month. If you add this amount to your other projected sources of income, you should be able to determine if this amount is indeed enough for you to live a comfortable life post-retirement.

As perfectly calculated as this may seem on paper, the 4% rule has its drawbacks too. Recently, experts have been skeptical of this, so that you may use this as a starting point, but don't rely on this as the sole determinant of your retirement income and allowable withdrawals.

Step 3: Establishing a System to Track Your Finances

This is a tricky step, especially because many people believe that once they have created their retirement accounts and set the wheels in motion, they are all set. If only it were this easy! The point is, financial and economic conditions are constantly evolving, and without keeping track of those changes, you are heading straight for danger. It's crucial that you revisit your retirement budget every now and then.

It's also necessary that you balance your investment portfolio every now and then to see if you are on track to meet your retirement savings goals.

RETIREMENT IS ALSO ABOUT THE ATTITUDE

Though we have talked extensively about the technicalities of a retirement budget, retirement—or even finances, for that matter—doesn't happen in a vacuum. Much to the contrary, they happen in the rich context of your life, goals, ambitions, relationships, health, and so on and so forth, and they should be treated as such. I always tell my clients this: retirement specifically, or financial planning in general, is as much about your attitude as it is about the numbers. Before we get into the specific aspects of retirement planning, as detailed in the following chapters, I would like to talk to you about these core attitudinal changes that can get you across the line.

Pay Yourself First

I cannot stress enough how crucial this one principle is to your financial planning journey. And yet it's one that's often ignored. Think about it—what's the first thing that you do with your paycheck? Pay the bills, taxes, etc.? Well, don't worry; you are not the only one. But just because everyone does, it doesn't make it a good idea. If you are taking the leftovers of your earnings that you have worked so hard for, how motivating can it be, after all? Not at all!

The idea here is to avoid paying the government their share even before you receive your paycheck. No, I am not talking about any illegal activity here—this is something we have already spoken of in terms of 401(k), 403(b), IRAs, etc. These financial instruments allow you to legally avoid anywhere between 10-37% of taxes. A crucial aspect of this process is automation. If you think of doing all this manually, it can seem a tad overwhelming. Also, while doing it manually, you run the risk of just forgetting once in a while, and then the whole system fails.

Automating your finances, or rather, setting up your accounts in such a way that a particular portion of your paycheck is automatically redirected to pretax savings accounts, is particularly efficient. You no longer have the opportunity to make excuses as you don't even get to see the whole paycheck and have to make do with the amount available in your checking account. It is highly recommended that you automate your finances. What this means is that, rather than spending a considerable time at the beginning of every month trying to channel money in the right direction, make sure that the cuts happen automatically. So, even if you forget once in a while to do this, the system keeps running perfectly fine. Moreover, there's no excuse anymore, and you have to figure out a way to manage your expenses using the remainder of the paycheck.

But again, it's not just about these accounts and numbers. To me, *paying yourself first* goes much deeper than the simple behavior of pretax savings; I consider it an attitudinal shift that allows you to view your life entirely differently. I want you to ingrain this attitude in your mind. *Pay yourself first* is not just about how much money you are saving, but how much are you working for your and your family's sake? How much are you able to really keep for yourself and your loved ones?

On the face of it, *paying yourself first* may seem like an aphorism for self-indulgence. Many, upon reading this for the first time, may even mistake this to mean getting some reward for themselves. This couldn't be farther from the actual meaning of this powerful phrase. When you simply go on a spending spree in the name of rewarding yourself, you have relinquished your money and, therefore, still have no control. *Pay yourself first* isn't only a tax-saving technique; it's about having the freedom to decide what you want to do with your money in the long run, not just on an impulse. It's all about making sure the money you slog for actually stays with you rather than filling up the pockets of either Uncle Sam or someone else.

Imagine, for a moment, if every dollar you paid yourself today grew five times in the next 20 years! Go on—see what that would look like for you and your retirement! You can rest assured that this wealth can certainly grow five times by the time you decide to retire, maybe even more. Does that seem like a fantasy? Well, welcome to the magical world of *pay yourself first*, my friend!

Skipping on Savings Is Not an Option

One attitude toward money management that breaks my heart every single time is that financial planning is a fancy term only for the wealthy. I hear this more often than you might expect. People find it almost offensive when I talk to them about savings, their defense being, "We are hardly making ends meet! How do you expect us to save?!" If you pay attention, this attitude comes only as a consequence of not practicing the "pay yourself first" tenet. When you believe that savings can happen only from the leftovers of your paycheck, how are you going to save if there's nothing left at the end of the month?!

If that's how you feel, too, I have what you might consider good and bad news for you. The good news is that, regardless of your income, there is always something you can save. The bad news is, to save, you might need to give up some things dear to you—that cappuccino that you pick up from your nearby cafe, for instance, or that monthly subscription to the cable TV guide. Moreover, the tried and tested methods of persistent haggling and using coupons wherever possible can indeed save you a lot more than you'd expect. Now, I know that that seems like an austere life to live, but that kind of discipline might help you squeeze out the much more valuable savings bucks from your supposedly "un-saveable" paycheck. These small savings can accumulate into something significant over time.

You might think that people who make more money would surely be much better at savings. Well, unfortunately not! Judging by the fact that the more your income, the more your lifestyle expenses, even those that make a comfortable income tend to goof up their savings. They seem to be solely focused on the amount of money they have to spend rather than the percentage of the income they should be saving. Do you remember the 50/30/20 rule we discussed? 20% of every paycheck should go into savings. This would also include your retirement savings. Many feel like they are doing great on their savings report card simply because they have maxed out their 401(k). This is a grave fallacy because if you are making $200,000 and saving only $20,500 as allowed by your 401(k), then you are technically only saving about half of what you should be saving. The idea is not to retain a definite figure as savings but a percentage of your income.

Your Partner In Crime

The last, but just as detrimental attitude towards financial management, is that of segregating the financial responsibilities between spouses. Finances often become the territory of only one spouse who is "good at numbers and money matters" in general. They take care of budgeting, bills, taxes, and the retirement nest egg too. A study by UBS Global Wealth Management reports that though 82% of women view joint financial management as the right thing to do, only 51% actually participate in the financial decision-making in their household (UBS Media, 2020). What's even more unfortunate is that millennial women are more likely to defer their financial responsibilities to their spouses, suggesting that the upcoming generation of women are taking a less active interest in their finances, especially after marriage.

You may argue that such a division of labor may lead to better efficiency, as people with specific skills should take up the responsibilities matching those skills. While logical, absolute compartmentalization in this form is likely to do more harm than good. This harm is almost palpable in extreme cases of spousal death, abuse, divorce, etc. It's no secret that money matters are one of the most common areas of dispute among married couples. But even if you think none of that would ever happen to you—and I hope you are right—even in daily life, a disjointed approach to finances is not a good idea.

I completely agree that one of the two partners might be more adept with finances. While it's completely fine to let them take on these responsibilities, the other spouse must certainly be financially aware of where the money is coming from and where it is going. This is especially prudent in crises when the other spouse, for whatever reason, might need to make some critical financial decisions. I suggest that you sit with your spouse at the end of every month and do a sort of review of your finances. This may include your savings, expenditures, investments, etc. You can either use a free online net worth tracker like *Personal Capital,* which allows you to access your data in an interactive dashboard, or you can maintain your own manual spreadsheet with headings like:

- Cash
- Investments (stocks, mutual funds, etc.)
- Businesses
- Pensions
- Debt (mortgage, credit card debt, loans, etc.)
- Vehicles
- Real estate

You can then enter the returns and the expenses on all of these entries and assess them in their entirety in your month-end exercise.

THE BEGINNER'S RETIREMENT PLANNING CHECKLIST

- Create and adhere to a 50/30/20 budget
- Estimate your retirement income and create a retirement budget
- Make sure you have pretax savings in the form of 401(k), 403(b), etc.
- Do a monthly review of your budget as well as savings along with your partner.
- Automate your finances

HEALTH IS WEALTH

Give a man health and a course to steer, and he'll never stop to trouble about whether he's happy or not.

— GEORGE BERNARD SHAW

One of my clients—let's call him Robbie—has always been one of the rare, spectacularly financially prudent people that I have had the good fortune to work with. I met him when he was in his early 30s. At a time when most of us are only beginning to attain a fair understanding of adulthood and the long-term responsibilities it brings, this guy was spot on with his financial goals. He would budget regularly, knew precisely what he wanted, and followed all the advice I gave him to get there very religiously. For quite some time, things were going pretty smoothly for Robbie, but as I got to know him more, the perfect facade seemed to be evaporating one brick at a time. As much in awe as I was of his financial progress, I slowly learned that other areas of his life were not nearly as perfect. His marriage was unraveling, and he had an almost fatal heart attack at 38.

Since he had come to be more than just a client for me at this point, I went to see him in the hospital, and I could have sworn it was a different man in Robbie's body. This new version of Robbie told me how all he had done all his life was work and earn money and how in those moments when his heartbeat seemed to be slipping, he didn't even care about the savings and the investments. The only thing he cared about was how he had never taken a day off to spend with his family, or how he had never gone to see the majestic pyramids of Egypt that he had always wanted to see, or how he should have been a little kinder to himself, physically and emotionally. Toward the end, when I got up to leave, he called out to me, "Hey, Money Man!" That's what he used to call me fondly. "Maybe every once in a while, you should tell your clients to not just think about the money!"

And to this day, I have followed his advice. I make sure that, along with the financials, my clients are also paying attention to the big picture goals of their lives. Life, and more so, retirement, isn't only about the money in your account. As I said once before, it's about you—your health, goals, aspirations, relationships, and so on. All of this may feel a little out of place in a finance book, but if you ignore the big picture, even the best-laid financial plans can be razed to the ground.

A BALANCED LIFE

The younger generation is quite fond of this one phrase: YOLO—you only live once. I have, of course, seen youngsters go quite overboard with reckless risk-taking in the name of this phrase. But I also see that the so-called Baby Boomers and Gen X folks might do well to be reminded of this term every once in a while. We belong to the generations that have been conditioned to work, work, then work some more, accumulating money but never having the time to enjoy it. The reminder that we all only live once—that only working and earning money may not be the best way to spend all of our lives—might just help break the habit. Instead, focusing on yourself, first and foremost, might be the best investment you ever make.

Physical Health

Physical health is the first thing that comes to mind when we talk about 'health.' The culture that surrounds us is crazily and simultaneously stress-inducing and health-promoting. While on the one hand, we are flooded in our work lives with never-ending deadlines, on the other hand, we are also constantly shown visuals of healthy individuals living their best lives, laughing and enjoying all the way! What's more, this contradiction is not just limited to the perceptual level but is even seen in medical trends.

While stress-induced illnesses, both physical and psychological, are threatening our longevity more than ever, the advances in the medical field also ensure that we are living much longer than our ancestors. What do these trends mean for your physical health at this moment, though? Well, as confusing as these statistical conclusions may be, the best thing you can do for your health is to have a balanced lifestyle.

When we think of physical health and fitness, it's easy to get carried away by the chiseled bodies and the intricate workout routines that we are exposed to in the media. But this is not at all what I am talking about here. Remember, you don't need to be doing crossfit training to stay healthy, and eight-pack abs aren't necessarily a sign of fitness. The idea is to keep moving with a routine that is relatable and accessible for you. If Crossfit does that for you, great! If you are someone who likes to cycle, go ahead, do that. If you enjoy an evening stroll with your partner, then that is what you need to do.

When choosing a physical routine, remind yourself to keep away from the perpetrated notions of perfect health and do what's best for you. What I see happening around me most of the time is that people tend to get excited about health and fitness and devise these extravagant routines that they usually wouldn't follow. They give it their all the first few days, and then the zeal fades away, making them quickly return to their unhealthy old patterns.

Of course, there's no one right way to maintain fitness, and everyone needs to understand the activities they like to engage in (and also the ones that they hate) in order to come up with a routine that keeps them active while also helping them enjoy the moment. One thing I can say, though, is that tiny changes that are sustainable create much more impact than grand changes that you will give up on.

I'd like to reiterate here that I realize that talking about this in a financial planning book is quite unorthodox. But I see this as an essential part of our discussion, not only because I consider it the best investment but also because I see people overwhelmed by where to start. When it comes to physical health, there are multiple avenues that you can take, and this itself can lead to further procrastination. Don't try to do it all at the same time—that's the most significant mistake people make. Take a look at the following suggestions:

- early morning / late night jogs
- a 45-minute walk
- yoga and meditation
- hiking and trekking
- cycling
- swimming
- playing your favorite sport
- dancing
- going to the gym

There are many other things that you can do to keep yourself on the move; note those down if you wish. Now, pick one activity and answer the following questions:

1. If I had to rate my love for this activity on a scale of 1 to 10, how high would I rate it?
2. Why this activity? What is it about this routine that excites me?
3. How can it benefit me physically and emotionally?
4. When do I plan to perform this activity every day, and for what duration?
5. What is my goal in regards to this? For instance, if running is the activity I picked, then maybe I'll run a marathon at some point or even simply run for 45 minutes or a certain number of miles.
6. What is the smallest step I can take towards creating a lasting routine around this activity?

Only when you have honestly answered these questions will you be able to assimilate it into your daily life. Once you are comfortable and consistent with one activity, you can go ahead and incorporate more if you so wish. But remember not to go overboard by trying to do everything! The important thing is that you are deriving the physical benefits of these active routines but also that you are able to draw positivity from them. These activities shouldn't in themselves become another source of stress.

Just as a car would require routine servicing as well as fuel to be able to run smoothly, so does our body. While physical exercise is the service, your diet and sleep are the fuel for the vehicle that is your body. Remember, your output will always be proportional to your input, so what you put inside your body will directly determine how your body will perform in the long run.

Many of my clients have a strenuous work life; they are constantly striving to accumulate the funds that will make their future better, all by severely compromising their present health. Since they are always on the go, they want to eat fast, sleep less, and work more. As your body goes through the wear and tear of growing old, you can be sure that it will become less and less tolerant of these erratic schedules. Thus, if we are to have a healthy retirement, we must pay attention to not just our physical activity but also our diet and sleep.

Let's take a moment to think about your diet first. As with everything else, there are virtually infinite ways you can approach bringing about changes in your diet —the vegan diet, Keto, Paleo, Mediterranean, the list goes on and on. Depending on your preferences, you can pick and choose the diet that works best for you. Whatever you choose, remember that the goal is not to have an ultra-strict regimen or stay at a particular weight. The goal is to be healthy and to feel good in your body—and not necessarily to stick to the social convention of the perfect weight. Also, remember, crash diets don't serve any purpose apart from making you feel miserable. Besides, since weight loss is not our goal, you can toss those diets out straight away without a second thought. Make sure your diet is balanced and has ample ingredients that allow you to enjoy the morsels that you put in your mouth. Moreover, this diet doesn't have to have some fancy name either. As long as you are getting enough of all the food constituents, you are good to go. Of course, if you do have any pre-existing conditions, it's essential to talk to your doctor before making any dramatic changes in either your physical workout routine or the diet that you consume.

The last aspect that you need to focus on is getting enough sleep. Be it the pressure of our responsibilities or our addiction-like attachment to our phones; our sleep is among the first to be put on the sacrificial altar. Did you know that most of the growth that happens in babies occurs when they sleep? That is the reason babies tend to sleep a lot more than adults. Even as we grow older, sleep performs some really important functions and helping us rest isn't even the most crucial of them. The growth hormone released during sleep is responsible for repairing the wear and tear that your body has experienced all day. If not given the required time to do this, the body would never be able to over-come its stressed state, leading to perpetually elevated levels of cortisol, the stress hormone. Without going into the biological depths of it all, we all know that stress can, in turn, significantly impact our metabolism. This means that no matter what you eat and how much you work out, until and unless you get enough sleep, the body will never be able to reap the full benefits of all these measures. Again, if you experience inconsistencies in your sleep patterns because of conditions like insomnia, sleep apnea, etc., the best thing to do is to consult your doctor.

Mental and Emotional Well-Being

Often, we get so immersed in maintaining our physical health that we completely forget the very aspect that may be fueling our bad physical health indirectly—our mental and emotional states of mind and our psychological health. By now, we know the role that mental wellness plays in our overall well-being. But despite knowing this, it's common to see people take their mental health for granted. This conditioning that we have been subjected to must break today—more than ever. Your mind will not automatically keep up with the stress that you throw at it. Investing in strengthening your mental core is just as important as (if not more important than) working on that physical core. Of course, the separation between physical and mental wellness is only for the purpose of our understanding. In reality, both tend to have a cyclical impact on each other. It's crucial to understand this cyclical nature, especially if post-retirement wellness is your goal.

I find the concept of lifespan development in psychology quite interesting. It can even prove relevant to financial planning. Lifespan development explores the different stages of human development and the changing needs of the individual at each stage. When planning for retirement, it's paramount that we understand what to expect when we enter this particularly vulnerable stage. Sure, retirement may bring freedom from responsibility, but it also very likely brings about a gradual loss of skills and restriction of movement that you have never experienced before. Considering this, it would be wise to slow this natural decline in cognitive and muscular capacities as much as possible. How can you do that, you ask? Well, by keeping mentally active as much as possible.

The best way to keep mentally active is to keep busy. Busy can either mean you are engaging in that part-time employment we spoke about earlier or that you are taking this leisure time to devote to your hobbies, the ones you always complained of not having enough time for. One hobby that people invariably put off until retirement is travel. A little heads-up, though—the fantasy of enjoying exotic travel when you are older might be ridden with several practical difficulties. First off, you never know if you'll want to travel to all those places when you are older. Secondly, no one's seen what's around the corner, so why not grab this moment and take that road trip you have so badly wanted to take?! After all, now is the only time there is! Instead, I say, go ahead and make a bucket list of all the places you have wanted to visit—near, far, doesn't matter—the Northern Lights, the Pyramids, the Bahamas, traveling around Japan, backpacking across Europe, whatever it is, stop postponing it! Enjoy your life in the moment rather than procrastinating about it.

Keeping mentally busy is not all about travel and shenanigans, though. Strengthening your mental faculties for your post-retirement phase also requires that you sharpen your cognitive skills and engage your brainpower with as many activities as possible. But guess what, these activities don't have to be boring at all because, at the end of the day, it's all about creating new neural pathways by learning new things. Think about the following things to keep your brain active:

- solving puzzles
- learning a new language
- learn and teach a new skill

- practice empathy
- build relationships
- playing chess, card games, etc.
- develop a hobby

Engaging with your brain is particularly important when planning for retirement. You may feel like retirement is the best time to kick back and relax. While this may be an excellent plan, research suggests that taking too much time off can actually be harmful to you. It eventually comes down to the "use-it-or-lose-it" principle. A study even points to the finding that early retirement may cause an earlier decline in cognitive function than late retirement. This does not mean that you need to work your job all your life, but it's essentially about not allowing retirement to get in the way of you being a dynamic, growing, learning individual.

Health and Healthcare

As we see above, the health of retirees can seem like a bleak issue, but it's a matter of significant importance nevertheless. This importance is not only at an individual level but also at the national policy-making level. This is why there are multiple studies across nations that examine this stage of lifespan development in painstaking detail. The English Longitudinal Study of Aging (ELSA) in the UK and the Health and Retirement

Study in the USA are just a couple of examples of such longitudinal studies that interview older adults after a defined time period; in both these cases, after every couple of years.

Though the specific results in these studies might vary, overall, researchers in this arena seem to be divided in their opinions as to whether retirement bodes well for the health of the retirees or not. Some are of the opinion that retirees tend to have better health because of the absence of the mental and physical pressures of deadlines and responsibilities. On the other hand, another group of researchers believes that people's health tends to deteriorate due to the stress of reduced income.

Whichever it is, one thing is for certain—how you have lived your life prior to your retirement will have a significant impact on how you live through your retirement. Surprisingly, one of ELSA's findings has been that almost 60% of the surveyed aging population described their health as better than average, even excellent on some occasions (Ashurst, 2009.) But this isn't a natural consequence of growing up. These people have probably spent a considerable time and effort keeping their health that way. But here's the thing —you'd expect that being one of these uber-healthy individuals would reduce your healthcare expenses.

And it does in the short run, but in the long run, being healthy also increases the likelihood that you will live a long life. So, if you have been paying attention, you might just realize that building up a healthy lifestyle prior to retirement and establishing sufficient health-care funds for after retirement are two sides of the same coin, and both deserve your care and attention.

As you may have guessed, healthcare is the highest cost you can expect in retirement. Depending on where you are, healthcare costs will vary greatly. The US stands on top of that list, with $10,586 being spent per person annually—and that doesn't even include long-term care. In such cases, planning for appropriate coverage is paramount. If you are in the USA, you might want to gain as much awareness about Medicare as possible. As this Medicare comes in four parts, retirees are often confused about whether or not they require all of them.

Without going into too many details, for our purposes, it will suffice to identify the following parts of Medicare.

Part A: Hospital coverage

Part B: Medical services and supplies

Part C: Special advantage plans like those covering special needs, preferred providers, health maintenance, and even added services like dental, wellness, vision, etc.

Part D: Prescription drugs

If you will be dependent on Medicare, it would indeed be wise to plan for some costs out of your own pocket, like premiums and deductibles, because typically, Medicare does not cover all expenses. While Part C payments will vary depending on the plan, consider these deductibles and premiums for Medicare Part A, B, and D as they stand at present in 2022 (Lake, 2021):

- The standard deductible for Part A: $1,556
- The standard monthly premium for Part B: $170.10
- The standard annual deductible for Part B: $233
- The standard monthly premium for Part D (may vary according to income): $33

A significant loophole in the Medicare plan is that it doesn't cover long-term care. This may be mitigated by taking out a long-term care insurance plan, which may limit your costs to the monthly premiums but may end up saving you a lot of your precious dollars if the need for long-term care arrives.

I know that those figures can build up to something substantial over time and can feel like a drain on your finances. But one thing you can be certain of is that paying for proper health care is worth every penny you put in. There are other options too that you can explore to pay for your healthcare. If you have not yet registered for Medicare, health savings accounts (HSAs) offer tax advantages along with high-deductible health plans. The funds that you save up in these accounts can be used to cover the Medicare premiums when you enroll.

Your health and well-being are invaluable, and you cannot afford to treat them any less than that. So, do not hesitate to spend on something that's aimed at keeping you healthy. Because, ultimately, that is an investment definitely worth making!

HEALTHCARE CHECKLIST

- Keep physically active—even if it's for 30 minutes a day, do it in the form that's most relatable to you.
- Have a balanced diet that's healthy and enjoyable in equal measure

- Don't delay your hobbies until retirement; do them NOW!
- Improve cognitive skills by engaging in a variety of tasks that keep you on your toes, alert, and learning.
- Make sure you get a good healthcare plan— read the fine print to ensure it's the best one for you.
- Most importantly, do not procrastinate your joy!

OF SAVINGS AND INVESTMENTS

There are no right or wrong answers; there is only intuition.

— TOM FORD

In life, the decision is rarely to choose between right and wrong; instead, you will often be faced with the choice between right and right, especially in the world of financial planning. When exploring savings and investments, especially from the retirement planning perspective, there are several options available to you. And interestingly, very few will be completely wrong for you. This means that a majority of the approaches will have some benefit or other for you. But this is the tricky part—just because it fetches you *some* benefit doesn't mean it's the best approach for you.

Most people engaging in retirement planning seem to have what they consider a safe, low-risk outlook. While a low-risk approach is great, the question that needs to be asked but is often skipped is, is the low-risk approach also leading to low growth for you? Don't get me wrong, I'm not an advocate of reckless risk by any standard, but when I see many people's overly cautious retirement planning approaches, it reaffirms my belief that retirement isn't about finding a good enough plan. As I said, at this stage, that would be setting the bar relatively low. Retirement is about finding the *best* plan for you, one that fulfills your maximum requirements, one that fits seamlessly like a puzzle piece to complete your retirement finances.

Investors are constantly on the lookout for an investment that is low-risk, provides great returns, and is effective in saving taxes. Unfortunately, though, such a Utopic investment is yet to be discovered. So, all you can do for now is to create a well-balanced portfolio that eventually allows you to enjoy all these characteristics to different extents. For instance, mutual funds may satisfy the low-risk criteria, individual stocks may give great returns, and tax-deferred accounts like the

401(k) might be best for being tax-efficient. At the end of the day, it's all about choosing the right investments and the right accounts to hold those investments.

In this chapter, I'd like to take you through the major milestones of the investment journey so that you can create your own roadmap and set forth on this adventure. Remember that I will not be prescribing ready-made solutions here. Think of this chapter, and this book in general, as a pantry full of wonderful ingredients. It's up to you to take your favorite ingredients and cook a meal that satisfies all your senses.

CHOOSING THE RIGHT ACCOUNTS

Taxes are the first thing to think of when planning your finances for retirement. We can fantasize all we want about how great life would be without having to pay these taxes, but at the end of the day, we just have to accept the fact that Uncle Sam is going to take a sizable bite out of your paycheck. Though this puts a significant restriction on our ability to save at a fast pace, we aren't left completely helpless. As we mentioned in the context of the *pay yourself first* principle, there are, of course, ways to avoid these taxes and accelerate your savings rate as much as possible.

Yes, we are talking about retirement accounts. These retirement accounts are so critical in financial planning that we have to discuss them in much more detail. Also, it would be useful to note that every country has a different taxing system and, consequently, differently structured tax benefits as well. While what we discuss in this book is largely applicable to the United States, I strongly urge you to find the equivalent to these in your own country.

There are two common retirement accounts that can help you save on taxes: tax-exempt and tax-deferred. Both of these accounts are incredibly effective in reducing your taxes. This in itself can be an excellent motivation for you to start channeling to a neat piggy bank those dollars that would have been spent on paying taxes. The difference between these two is simply the time at which you can start availing yourself of the tax benefits. Having a detailed understanding of both of these is crucial in order to decide which one applies to you.

Having a tax-deferred account means that the tax advantage would begin right away. Any funds directed to these accounts remain tax-free, helping you grow your investments without the burden of giving some to the government. The subsequent withdrawals, when they do happen, however, would be taxed at the regular income rate. The logic behind this is simple—you're likely to have a lower income during your old age, resulting in a lower income bracket and thus an obligation to pay lower taxes. Thus, if you have a high income right now, it would make total sense to max out your tax-deferred accounts.

The most popular tax-deferred accounts are 401(k)s and traditional IRAs. Of course, these accounts don't allow for unlimited contributions; as of 2022, you can put in a maximum of $20,500 into your 401(k) and a maximum of $6,000 into your IRA. Let's say your annual taxable income is $85,000. If you max out your 401(k) with $20,500, then you would be required to pay tax only on $64,500. Fast forward to your retirement days. Let's say your taxable income is $60,000, and you decide to withdraw $4,000 from your 401(k). Then your total taxable income would be only $64,000.

Furthermore, when you invest in your tax-deferred accounts, you also receive a tax refund as per the tax rate. So, if you pay a tax rate of 32% and you channel $4,000 into your 401(k), you'll receive a refund amounting to $1,280 (0.32 x 4000), which means you can now invest the original $4,000 plus the refund of $1,280, which comes to a grand total of $5,280.

Tax-exempt accounts, on the other hand, don't provide a tax benefit when the contribution is made but rather when the funds are withdrawn. Remember that these are not pre-tax savings accounts and are beneficial only in terms of letting the returns on your investments— and not the investments themselves—grow tax-free. Roth IRAs and Roth 401(k)s fall into this category. This path to savings is usually recommended for individuals who have a low income at present and are expected to fall into a higher income bracket sometime in the future. For instance, young adults who have just joined the workforce may have minimal earnings at the moment, which means the taxes they save right now would also be negligible. However, in the future, when your taxes are likely to climb significantly, the previously opened tax-exempt accounts may help you reduce taxes considerably. These accounts are especially beneficial when you expect the value of your investment to appreciate over time. For instance, if you invest in mutual funds through a tax-exempt account, the returns that it gathers over the years will be tax-free too.

In a nutshell, when choosing between tax-deferred and tax-exempt accounts, you need to consider the purpose for which you are choosing them. If retirement planning is your sole aim, then I strongly recommend that you explore your tax-deferred account options. On the other hand, if your goal is a long-term investment, then tax-exempt accounts might be your best bet. Again, different countries may name these retirement schemes differently. For example, in the United Kingdom, you might want to look into the option of an Individual Savings Account (ISA), whereas in Canada, the Registered Retirement Savings Plan (RRSP) might be more popular. All said and done; however, your own research regarding your financial needs and the financial plans available in your location will prove to be of prime importance.

The 401(k) Plan

We have used this term multiple times now, but many who hear this term all the time still have their doubts about what it really is. This is a retirement plan that's popular among quite a lot of American employers. In this plan, you basically agree to divert a certain percentage of your salary into tax-advantaged retirement savings. The employer has the option to match either part or the whole of this contribution. Again, the 401(k) may be either traditional (tax-deferred) or Roth (tax-exempt). Here are a few things to remember about these plans:

- The maximum contribution to both traditional and Roth 401(k) is $20,500. If you are over 50 years of age, you might have to do some catch-up with your contribution, and the usual

$20,500 maximum would be increased to
$26,500.

- The employee-employer contributions cannot
  go beyond $61,000, and for employees over 50,
  the limit is set at $67,500.

- Employers can not contribute to a Roth 401(k),
  only a traditional 401(k).

- Withdrawing from a 401(k)—traditional or
  Roth—before the age of 59½ years is a bad idea.
  While technically, you do have the option of
  taking out a loan on your retirement savings, it
  should really be the absolute last resort. These
  loans would have to be paid back with interest,
  and it's generally difficult to take out these
  funds without the withdrawals becoming
  taxable. There is also a 10% penalty on
  withdrawals made earlier than the prescribed
  age.

- It is mandatory for you to withdraw a certain
  percentage of the savings in the account after
  72 years of age. This is called "required
  minimum distributions" (RMDs).

- Since your employer is the most accessible
  means to open a 401(k), leaving your job also
  has some implications for the account. While
  some employers may allow you to keep your
  401(k) going even if you take up a new job, you

may also explore other options like rolling your 401(k) into an IRA, moving it to the new employer, or if you have reached the permitted age, you might even consider withdrawing the funds.

- A solo 401(k) might work for you if you are self-employed. Through this plan, you can make a contribution to your account as both an employee and an employer, which allows you to accumulate larger sums in savings. Just remember, if you make a contribution to your own account as an employer, you have to follow suit for all other employees too.

GAUGING YOUR RISK TOLERANCE

Returning to what we discussed at the beginning of the chapter, retirement planning is about the right balance between risk and growth. But the question that has most people befuddled is: where do you draw that line? In my observation, most of these people prefer to put their savings and investments on autopilot and, thus, not having taken the time to understand the basics, are always thrown off by the process of financial planning.

Of course, everyone's needs and preferences are unique. I encourage my clients to take a more hands-on approach, especially when it comes to simple investments that they can take care of themselves, even without my help. Two questions that are extremely helpful in determining the direction of your investments are:

1. What kind of timeline are you looking at for your investment goals? Short-term, long-term, medium-term?
2. What is your risk tolerance? Based on the goals and your expected returns, are you planning to take an aggressive, risky approach or a safer one? Ultimately, it comes down to the surplus funds you have to digest the loss if indeed there is any.

No matter what financial experts say, you can be sure that each portfolio is as unique as the individuals themselves. Depending on your answers to the above two questions and also how hands-on you wish to be, your portfolio might be conventional in some sectors and aggressive in others. Rarely would you be a completely aggressive or a completely traditionally leaning investor. Either way, I suggest that you get an in-depth understanding of what you are investing in and why.

Before we go ahead, it might be beneficial to understand the term "asset class," as it is quite closely related to investments as well as risk tolerance. As you may be aware, your investment can take several forms. Some of these are quite similar to each other with respect to the laws that regulate them and also in terms of how they behave in the marketplace. These have thus been grouped together as one asset class. Some common asset classes, for instance, are currencies, real estate, equities such as stocks, and fixed income such as bonds. While the instruments in the same asset class likely behave similarly to each other, separate asset classes tend to behave quite differently from each other and sometimes may even be inversely correlated with each other. Diversification of your portfolio would thus involve assimilating different asset classes so that even if you are making losses with one asset class, the loss is usually mitigated by another asset class. This is in line with modern portfolio theory, which looks for that sweet spot that allows you to bring together different investment instruments that maximize your returns while minimizing your risk.

Most people I came across earlier in my career used to be quite uncomfortable with the financial market. However, I have seen that trend shift gradually over the past few years as more and more people seem curious about the markets as an investment tool to increase their income.

Individual Stocks

Even though stock markets and trading are commonly used in the financial planning arena, many still remain unclear about what a stock really is. Well, to put it simply, a stock is nothing but a fractional ownership of a particular company. This equity in the company is sold by the company to raise funds for its operations. Hence, owning shares (units of the stock) makes you entitled to receive the profits proportionate to your shares.

Individual stocks and shares are the playing field for an investor who wants to engage with their investments on a regular basis. They scour the markets for individual investments that can help them reap returns that take them closer to their financial goals. Stock investments have low costs as they eliminate the annual fees to the fund company for the investment of your assets. With stocks, you only have to pay fees when you buy or sell. Investing in the stock market also gives you a high degree of control over your investment portfolio. You can pick and choose your preferred stocks after thoroughly researching their backgrounds and performance.

Of course, stocks aren't without their flaws. To start with, a beginning stock investor will find it difficult to truly diversify their portfolio. This is because proper diversification requires that you own anywhere between 20 to 100 stocks (depending on which financial expert you follow), and this can be quite a challenge with limited funds. The time period for which you wish to own the stock is also of prime importance—only think of investing in a stock if it's for a minimum of five to ten years.

Also, remember that stock trading isn't about intuition. You can not wake up one fine day and decide to invest in stocks on an impulse. That is a sure-shot recipe for disaster. Scoring good returns requires that you invest considerable time in doing technical and fundamental analyses of the stocks and companies involved. That is not to say that it cannot be done, but as I mentioned before, it means that you would have to be much more involved in the process with both your time and energy.

Index Funds

Index funds are a type of mutual fund. At the risk of massively oversimplifying it, I like to think of individual stocks versus mutual funds as like the comparison between making your own flower bouquet or getting one from the florist. While in the former, you pick your favorites, in the latter, you let the florist—who you believe has expertise in which flowers would look best together—put together a bouquet for you.

Index funds are a step ahead. Index funds, in particular, have a portfolio that keeps track of the constituents of the financial markets. This means that these funds imitate the performance of an index, which is the whole stock market or at least broad segments of it. Here, there is no human involvement, and the fund simply mimics the benchmark of the index. They are what financial experts call "passively managed funds."

These are considered perfect for retirement planning because, as estimated by Warren Buffet as well, these index funds give the investor the opportunity to buy all of the stocks at a low cost. Standard & Poor's 500 Index (S&P 500) is a popular index fund that follows the biggest 500 stocks trading on the New York Stock Exchange (NYSE) and Nasdaq. Thus, more or less, this index fund acts as a tool to assess the performance of some of the biggest American companies. The broad exposure that the investor gains comes at little risk and low operating expense; in most cases, less than 0.20%, while competing actively managed funds may charge more than 1% in fees. This proves to be a perfect setting for those planning for retirement.

However, here again, your response to the first question we asked earlier about the timeline you are looking at would determine whether this investment instrument is for you or not. Passively managed funds have been shown to earn better returns than actively managed mutual funds over the long term. On the other hand, if you are looking at a shorter timeline, actively managed mutual funds might be better. This is because index funds are not looking to book profits on short-term up-and-down swings. That is something actively managed funds seek to do. On the contrary, index funds only match the movement of the overall market by following both the risk and returns. The idea is that the market will always win, eventually—*eventually* being the keyword.

Just as index funds can be structured as mutual funds, as discussed above, they can also come in the form of exchange-traded funds (ETFs). In this arrangement, a financial firm manages a stock portfolio where each stock represents a percentage stake in the portfolio itself. So, if one stock makes up 2% of the index, the firm mimics this pattern by making that stock 2% of the portfolio.

Bonds

Bonds belong to the asset class of fixed income. This means that the investor lends the investment money to a borrower, and the returns are paid as periodic interest until maturity, after which the principal amount is also returned to the investor. A bond may be thought of as a contract between the two parties specifying the details of the loan and its repayment as well. Bonds are usually used by large organizations and governments. While investing in bonds, one would have to be cognizant of the borrower's background and the possibility that the borrower may default on the transaction. This is where the investor's risk tolerance comes in.

While bonds come in multiple forms and categories, I would like to point out here one specific asset which is considered particularly good for retirement—the treasury bond. These come with a minimum risk of default as they are issued and guaranteed by the U.S. Treasury. These come in two forms: treasury notes with short-term maturity terms—maybe two, three, five, seven, up to 10 years—and treasury bonds with a longer maturity of maybe 20 to 30 years. Though bonds generate lower returns than stocks, they still offer a steady stream of income that's pretty much risk-free.

Having said that, though, bonds also have some disadvantages. For instance, due to the economic crisis of 2020, the interest rates on issued bonds were slashed, and it would be beneficial to invest in them only if you expect the rates to climb. Sometimes, it may happen that, despite good planning, you might find yourself stuck with low-performing bonds until their maturity due to fluctuating interest rates.

Real Estate

It's quite possible that up until now, the only time you have looked into real estate is when you or your friends thought of buying a house. If that's the case, you are not the only one. Most people tend to think of real estate as an investment for the present and hardly as one for the future. Especially if you are not quite there with your retirement fund, investing in real estate may fetch you handsome returns. The timing of the purchase is of prime importance in cases like this.

On the whole, you can approach real estate investment in a few different ways. One of these is, of course, running rental properties. Here, you may just buy a property, make the necessary renovations, and then let tenants move in and pay you the rent. This is a great income opportunity for those who are skilled in some do-it-yourself (DIY) remodeling and, more so, patient enough to deal with tenants. If the former excites you but not the latter, you can even consider flipping houses, whereby you'd purchase an undervalued property, add value to it through remodeling, and then sell it within six months. Exploring those options would probably take a book of its own, but for our purpose, it will suffice to know that though this can help bring in a good income and is usually seen to be more profitable than the other passive investments we discussed above, real estate investment also requires quite a bit of work as well as considerable capital.

Most people in retirement wouldn't want to go through this hassle. But you need to make a choice as to what suits you the best. And if you plan to do this, you might want to start early. This is because rental property owners, as well as house flippers, tend to take out loans on their mortgage to purchase the initial property. Again, you'd need to have a steady job and income, as the banks tend to emphasize this.

If this doesn't seem like your thing, then don't worry. You aren't out of real estate options just yet. Two other options—Real Estate Investment Groups (REIGs) and Real Estate Investment Trusts (REITs)—might be more up to your speed. The REIGs allow the investor to gain the benefits of running a rental property without actually running it. An REIG is typically built by a company that allows investors to purchase a property from the set it has developed, thereby joining the REIG. While the investor rakes in a portion of the rent, the company does the job of handling tasks like maintenance of units and management of tenants. The management company is then given a percentage of the monthly rent. If you think about it, this is almost like hiring a manager for your rental property.

REITs, on the other hand, are better for those who want to have real estate in their investment portfolio without buying any actual property. REITs are much like individual stocks and can be bought and sold on the major exchanges. Here, a corporation utilizes the money from several investors to buy and manage properties. To keep the REIT status ongoing, the corporation would have to pay off 90% of its taxable profits as dividends to the investors. This ensures a steady stream of income for the investors while also keeping their investments quite liquid. These trusts allow individual investors to take a swing at corporate non-residential real estate like offices, malls, etc., which would be quite difficult to get into otherwise. If you are looking into REITs as an investment, you might want to be sure as to what kind of REITs they are—equity REITs that give you ownership in real estate or mortgage REITs that are more about gaining profits from mortgage financing.

The last approach to real estate investing is online real estate platforms, whereby the investor is allowed to take a bite out of bigger commercial and residential transactions. This is often known as real estate crowdfunding. This is indeed quite similar to crowdfunding as we know it in the corporate world, whereby an investor buying a stock would assume a fractional ownership in the company itself, thereby allowing the company to raise funds for its operations. In the same way, here, the individual wouldn't need to purchase the entire property but invest only in a fractional ownership of the property. This also gives them access to the profits earned by the property in the future in terms of rent or sale. This is especially beneficial for people planning for smaller investments, as they can become shareholders with as little as $5,000.

So, the times when real estate only meant buying and selling property are long gone, and now you have these multiple options at hand. The wise thing would be to assess each of these by comparing their expected returns to your own risk appetite and investment goals.

Annuities

Annuities as financial instruments are beneficial for retirement planning because of their assured returns, sometime in the future, usually after retirement. Annuities work in a couple of phases. The first is the accumulation phase, wherein the investor pays either a lump sum or periodic premiums. Once the first phase is over, then begins the annuitization phase with the payments by the financial institution kicking in for either some fixed period or for the rest of the annuitant's life, depending on the terms of the annuity.

Again, these may be immediate annuities or deferred annuities. Deferred annuities tend to grow in the tax-deferred accounts we saw earlier and are paid out after a date specified by the annuitant, whereas immediate annuities (also known as Single Premium Immediate Annuity or SPIA) are purchased with a lump-sum payment, and the payouts often start within the year. Immediate annuities may be a good idea if you have received a large amount of money, maybe from a settlement, the lottery, or even from your 401(k).

Remember that annuities are usually recommended for those who are closer to retirement and fear that they may run out of savings in their retirement. The regular income provided by the annuities is expected to keep them afloat. While this may look like a tempting prospect for an older individual, the same cannot be said of a younger investor. The money that's put into these annuities is illiquid, meaning that it cannot be cashed out when required, at least not without penalties. This may severely restrict the financial movement of a young investor, who may already have limited financial freedom.

Volatility and Risk Appetite

Now that we have looked at the most relevant asset classes for the purpose of retirement planning, it's also essential that we look at the flúctuations that these financial instruments are exposed to more often than not. Volatility refers to the steep and sometimes unpredictable price movements that the financial market or securities undergo from time to time.

Volatility often comes into focus only when prices fall, but the truth is, the upward movement of prices also counts as volatility. It's essential to understand this because we mostly tend to have a negative association with the word 'volatility,' believing that it only means an impending market crash. In reality, very profitable market jumps are also due to volatility. Moreover, investors know that just because a market crashes does not mean it's the end. If you are the one to pay close attention to the news, economic policies, etc., you can still make money by predicting the downward movement of the market.

Volatility is a complex statistical concept, but two types of volatility are particularly useful to you as an investor. Historical volatility looks at the past market prices and is expressed as a percentage increase or decrease in present prices compared to the past ones. Implied volatility is the second type that forecasts future movements of the market prices. Think of this in the stock market. In a bearish market where prices are expected to fall (because a bear swipes its paws down to attack its prey), the implied volatility generally increases, whereas, in bullish markets where prices are expected to rise (because a bull attacks by tossing the prey up on its horns), the implied volatility decreases.

Volatility and risk profiles are closely associated—the higher the risk, the greater the volatility, and also the greater the reward:

- The equity assets that we looked at in the form of individual stocks are quite volatile with a high-risk profile, but when done right, they also garner the best returns, especially when options and futures are traded.
- Real estate isn't as volatile as stocks and thus has a medium level of risk associated with it.
- Bonds also have a medium to high risk associated with them depending on the bond seller, except for government bonds, which are practically the safest investment you can make.
- Annuities aren't risk-free but tend to have a low-risk profile compared to stocks and bonds.
- Index funds are usually considered to have a low-risk profile despite being in the equity asset class, which is what makes them so popular.

Age and Asset Allocation

As you may have guessed from the above discussion, the allocation of assets in your portfolio is a dynamic concept that changes with time and your relative needs and risk appetite. With a low-risk appetite, you might invest much more conservatively and vice versa. Again, this should never be a test of intuition to determine what you 'feel' is right for you. Instead, I encourage my clients to keep all emotions out of the investment process. Determining your asset allocation with the help of a mathematical formula is particularly helpful in this regard. Don't worry now; this isn't some complex formula. All you have to do is to deduct your age from 100, and you can arrive at the percentage figure in your portfolio that should be dedicated to stocks. For instance, if you are 40 years old, then 40 subtracted from 100 would bring you to 60% of stocks in the portfolio and the rest in bonds.

DOING AWAY WITH THE DEBT

Having gained clarity on savings and investments thus far, it's time to get our hands a little dirty with one of the most controversial aspects of financial planning—debt. Many different financial experts will tell you many different things about debt. Some are completely against the idea of debt in all its forms and shapes, whereas others are much more liberal in this regard. Though I would like to think of myself as believing in "no debt is good debt," I also know that many can't afford to live a completely debt-free life. A mortgage is probably the most common example of such debt. How many do you know who can buy a house with money from their pockets? Not many, I'm sure. It's in cases like these that debt can serve a good purpose. However, such thought-out debt isn't the only kind that you come across. I am sure your credit card bills have made you wonder where you spent all that money and whether you really needed all or any of it! Now, that's a perfect example of bad debt.

In general, I'd consider any debt that helps you generate wealth, either by acquiring assets or by increasing your skills, to be good debt. So, education loans, business loans, and mortgages; these are all that may be considered good debts. On the other end of the continuum is debt taken to purchase commodities and consumables like cars, clothes, gadgets, etc. This is undoubtedly bad debt. These may be taken on credit cards, from loan sharks, or even as payday loans, and you can be sure that from start to finish, they are just a bad idea.

Remember that whether or not it's good debt, you must always aim to pay it off. Devise a system for debt management as it might be easy to forget about savings when clearing off debt or vice versa. Remember that if you pay off all your debt, leaving very little in your bank account, you might end up having to pay for your everyday items with your credit card, which would be an unhelpful loop. The idea is to create a budget that allows you to save, pay off debt, and have enough to cover your expenses. For instance, in the envelope system we discussed earlier, you might decide to add an envelope for debt too. You might not be able to channel a large amount to that envelope, and it might take a little longer to clear off the debt, but at least you have a system in place that allows you some certainty about your funds.

If you feel too overwhelmed with your debt, it might be wise to hire a financial advisor to help you assess your income streams and identify the problem areas. They can also help you narrow down potential courses of action you can take to best cope with the situation. But the decision to hire an advisor should not be taken lightly as they will also charge a fee, which might turn out to be an added drain on your resources. All in all, you have to do a thorough assessment of whether or not you can afford the hire; and if you feel like you can't do without the help, then consider how you can generate extra income to cover that expense in the future.

Savings and Investments Checklist

- Open a retirement savings account appropriate for your needs—be it a tax-deferred 401(k) or tax-exempt Roth 401(k) with your employer or an IRA or Roth IRA on your own.
- Determine your risk tolerance and investment timeline and start investing in appropriate assets.
- Create a budget that allows you to manage your debts effectively.
- Hire a financial advisor only if you feel you can not take it on by yourself.

4

OPTIMIZING YOUR PORTFOLIO

Good things happen to those who hustle.

— ANAIS NIN

I knew a woman—a mother of four and working. She worked as an assistant at a law firm. And had to get in before her boss every single morning. This meant that there were no calm mornings in her life. It was as chaotic as it could get. She and her husband would get the kids ready for school and pack their lunches. Her husband would then head to his work in his truck, and she would drop the kids off at school on the way to hers. Once she did this, however, she'd never go straight to work. She'd go to Starbucks, pick up a mocha frappuccino, and then sit sipping it in the park on the same bench every morning. That's how I met her. I'd see this lady in a visible hurry, prancing almost as she would go in and out of Starbucks, but the moment she reached her spot on the bench, she seemed to have been transported to a different, calmer world. One day, when I couldn't contain my curiosity, I asked her about the strange contrast in her body language when she was sitting on the bench and otherwise. She laughed heartily, told me about her schedule, and said, "My coffee and this bench keep me sane. And I need my sanity to go into work."

If ever this lady goes to a financial expert, the conventional advice she'd receive is to eliminate these coffees and other such activities, to pack her coffee from home if she really wants it, and save the precious $5. While this is all logical, I think it's a little excessive to pit savings and enjoyment against each other. Call me old school, but I believe there are things more precious in life than money. Of course, there may be times when you might have to give up more than what you bargained for in order to achieve a specific goal. But I am a little wary of making that the norm in life. Of course, everyone decides how they want to travel their financial journey, but all I am saying is you don't *have* to do it, and that's not the only way to have a happy retirement. Rather than saving up on meager expenses by cutting down on things you enjoy, I encourage my clients to think about increasing their income. Earning, let's say, an extra $30 a day would go much farther than saving $5.

After this chapter, I want you to be able to seriously consider the idea of starting a side hustle that makes the most of your unique abilities and creates a steady stream of income that reduces your complete reliance on your job to pay the bills.

THE NEED FOR A SIDE HUSTLE

Consider this person named Nick: he absolutely loves his job. It gives him not only money but also the job satisfaction that everyone talks about. He has just scored a promotion and is indeed quite happy with how his life is going. Then there's this guy called Shane, who used to work in the cubicle just next to Nick's before he got the promotion. He absolutely hates his job; he can't get any of his projects completed within a deadline, and, of course, his bosses aren't very happy with him. Now let me ask you a question—who among these two men needs a side hustle? Most of you would say Shane, obviously. With a job that's hanging by a thread, he really needs something of his own if he is to survive! Well, let me tell you, Shane certainly needs a side hustle, but he isn't the only one that needs it.

Our general perception is that a side hustle is for people who aren't entirely sure about their jobs. This is a myth perpetrated by the system that tells you to be a good kid, get good grades, get a good job with a fat paycheck, get married, have kids, and retire. The truth is, everyone needs a side hustle, no matter how successful they are at their day jobs. And well, to be honest, you are much more than a product of this conditioning. So, ask yourself if you'd like a backup income. If the answer you receive is yes, then side-hustles are for you. Of course, you'd be a victim of yet another myth if you believed that profitable side hustles just *happen to lucky people*. No, they don't. It's all about consistently working towards what you choose as your side hustle.

Choosing the Right Hustle

I firmly believe in making the most of working life and have found that side hustles are a great way to do that. They keep you productive, engaged, and financially independent. But despite them being perfectly comple-mentary to all that we have been talking about for our retirement planning, only a few manage to get their hustles off the ground. Many people have brilliant ideas, but only a few turn those ideas into effective side hustles. If not the ideas, then what stops these people from earning an income from their ideas, then? Well, in my experience, it's mostly the "money doesn't grow on trees" mindset. Even before they think about doing something with their ideas, they get bogged down with all the things they don't have—the time, the experience, the money. Let me tell you, and you don't need any of that to find a hustle that works for you. All you need is an idea that can generate money and the will to work for it.

Even if one moves past these fears, the next stumbling block is the all-too-common where-to-start conundrum. Mapping out a few criteria here can be extremely helpful as they keep us on track to success:

1. The what: The first question to get past is, "What do you choose to be your hustle?" How do you determine, out of all those ideas, which would be the one to change your life? Screening those ideas can in itself be a tough task to get through, especially because sometimes we tend to be rigidly attached to our ideas. It might help to have a better, more objective screening system in place.

In his book *Hustle* (2016), the author Neil Patel succinctly portrays what he calls "the hustler's sweet spot." Think of this as a four-quadrant system that holds all of your ideas:

a) Easy to comprehend, easy to perform: These are the ideas that everyone can take forward. There's nothing unique or proprietary about them. Because of this, the rewards that follow these ideas would be quite limited, if any.

b) Difficult to comprehend, easy to perform: This would include any ideas that lead you to learn new skills that may not be easy for people to acquire, but once acquired, they can be quite easy to perform. These could be beneficial, mainly because not all can persist through the learning curve.

c) Difficult to comprehend, difficult to perform: These may be the ideas that are tremendously difficult to both understand and perform. Think of becoming a neurosurgeon; the slightest error could be life-threatening. Despite the high rewards, it might not be something to be done lightly.

d) Easy to comprehend, difficult to perform: This is where things get interesting for people trying to start a side hustle. These are things that everyone can understand, but not everyone does, mainly because they call for discipline, patience, and persistence. This is where you have the chance to race past the pessimists and come up with something that gives you an edge over the majority of the population.

With this system in place, I strongly recommend that you sit down with a notepad and brainstorm a little about what your side hustle could be. When you have a list of these ideas, put them through the scanner of this screening system. You might just end up finishing this activity with an idea that could change your life.

2. The what *not*: While it's certainly important to think of what ideas could work for you, it's also necessary to have a cautionary note about the ideas that could derail your side hustle project. Often, when we look at a job and side hustle side by side, we tend to think of the former as an obligation to bring in the green and the latter as this tremendous passion project that fulfills every bit of your being. Needless to say, this is an overly simplistic and idealized perception. Be clear about what you want your side hustle for—if increasing income is your objective, then it's crucial that your passion doesn't sidetrack the main objective.

Of course, it's never recommended that you do something that you dislike just for the sake of money. But going to the other extreme may also act as a hindrance. While it's great to do something that impacts you emotionally, a deep emotional connection with something that you are trying to make money from may hamper your objectivity in improving your skills. Moreover, remember that your passions are subject to change just as you yourself change through time. And having an income stream based on your interests, which are subject to change, may not be the best idea either.

3. The how: When choosing your side hustle, it's imperative that you choose to do something that you already have the skills for. This is simply because if you hope to make money out of a hustle, then it needs to be of a certain quality. For instance, if I have no practical skills in graphic design, it just cannot be my side hustle even if I have theoretical knowledge of it. Understand that I am not emphasizing prior experience here but just your ability to create a great product that satisfies your customer. If you have always wanted to be a photographer and have only recently learned how to operate a camera, it might not do you much good at all. Sometimes people go overboard in identifying the most profitable hustle but underestimate the time that it will take them to master it. Sure, you can continue to gain new skills and turn them into future hustles, but you will have to make the difficult but objective decision of whether or not your skills are hustle ready.

4. The when: This is not really something you should have to figure out because the answer, regardless of what you choose to do, is *now*. If you have been thinking of starting up a tutoring gig, stop procrastinating and do it now. And the only real way to do that is to escalate your commitment. If you want to take up a DJing gig, make space in your budget for investing in the equipment. Making a financial commitment is much more likely to get you to stop procrastinating and get your hands dirty, actually doing what you want to do. Also, if this is the vision of yourself that you are putting out there and you are really committing to it in all ways you can, then subconsciously, you are much more likely to work towards it.

TRACKING AND REBALANCING YOUR PORTFOLIO

Increasing your income can drastically change the timeline of your retirement goals—more income means more savings, and more savings, of course, means either an upgrade in your retirement plans or the possibility of retiring early. This would come with a few cautionary notes, though, because retiring early isn't all that it's made out to be; it's not as glamorous, and as multiple research studies have shown us, it may not even be good for your health. But more on that later.

For now, let's focus on changing retirement goals. One thing to note is that we'll never know if our goals have changed until and unless we are vigilantly tracking our finances. We already spoke about apps like Personal Capital that help you with the tracking process. Now, let's take it one step further and tailor our portfolio based on our financial analysis. As we move through this section, I'd like you to also remember what we discussed about age and asset allocation percentages. Those will certainly come in handy when tracking our finances and rebalancing the portfolio.

I want you to be comfortable with the numbers of it all, which is something that turns off most people. So, let's play around with numbers a little to see what rebalancing would really look like. You may remember that using a mathematical formula; we arrived at the conclusion that at 40 years of age, the right balance would include 60% stock investment with 40% in bonds. That means that if you had $100,000 in your portfolio, $60,000 should be invested in stocks and $40,000 in bonds. But the thing to remember is that these figures do not remain constant. By the time you are 45, for instance, your portfolio may expand to, let's say, $175,000 with $50,000 in bonds and $125,000 in stocks. According to the formula we saw earlier; you'd now have to hold 55% rather than the previous 60% in stocks, which comes to $96,250. Thus, you currently have substantially more in stock than is advisable.

Rebalancing would involve selling a few stocks to reduce your stock investment to $96,250 and buying a few bonds to bring the investment in them up to $78,750. When selling stocks for gains, be sure to sell them in your retirement account so as to gain the tax benefits, whatever they may be. Some may argue, "But why ruin a good thing? If I am making good money on stocks, then why turn to a reduced reward in the form of bonds?!" Well, the idea, as we discussed before, too, is about risk management. Though it may not seem like it when things are going well, on bad days, it takes very little for things to go completely against you. And as retirement comes closer, your ability to absorb these bad days financially may become more and more restricted. Thus, you must think of rebalancing your portfolio at least once a year. I know it seems like a lot of work, but it's worth all the time and effort.

ACCELERATING YOUR RETIREMENT INCOME

There's no doubt that life puts to test the best-laid plans, many of which, unfortunately, doesn't emerge as winners. Often, you will be faced with life events that are completely outside your control, like death and sickness, and some—despite being in your control—

will still throw your budget off course, like the decision to have a wedding or children. No matter what you do, you might need to engage in a fair bit of course correction in retirement planning as well—sometimes getting to your goals quicker than you expected, sometimes having to take a long detour. Whichever it is, it's important to not give up midway and keep readjusting as you go.

The AARP calculator, which is a resource provided by the American Association of Retired Persons, is quite helpful in determining how such pit stops in your journey change your retirement goals. Go ahead, Google it and try experimenting with some numbers there. As you do this, you will realize that the higher your age at retirement, the fewer retirement finances you will require. So, those who fantasize about retiring early would require a significantly higher amount in their bank accounts to cover their expenses in retirement. On the other hand, those who retire later would need a smaller nest egg.

There are two factors to this. One, postponing your retirement would mean that most of the financially draining life events like buying a house, getting married, and having kids, have already happened—if you choose to stick to the conventional standards, that is. This would mean that finances required in the later stage of your life will be limited to things like health-care or some conscious life choices that you make. Second, and this is something that many fail to consider—regardless of life events, retiring early implies that you will spend more time in retirement too. So, a person retiring at 40 might have to think of the next 50 years of retirement (maybe even more), while one retiring at 70 would have to consider more or less only a couple of decades.

Channeling the extra money from your side hustle into retirement savings can make the process feel like a breeze, but just maxing out your retirement accounts will not be enough. So, what do you do? Well, I know we have spoken of retirement accounts in absolute reverential terms so far (and every word is true), but that doesn't mean that taxable accounts are all that bad. In fact, financial experts often point out that making your index fund investments through taxable accounts doesn't generally produce taxable capital gains. The point is if you have enough money coming in, maxing out your 401(k) is neither a point of pride nor an excuse to blow off the rest of your money. Watch your retirement goals like a hawk and persevere in making those savings even in the face of difficulties, or even more so in the face of temptations.

CHANGING THE MENTALITY TOWARDS RETIREMENT

We have discussed at length the types of investments that can help you create wealth and generate steady cash flow. We have long passed the days when interest and dividend payouts would be sufficient to maintain a good retirement lifestyle, and it's your unconventional cash flow that will keep you going in the end. As great as it is to be enthusiastic about these income streams, you also must be patient with them. Most people try something out for a while and then simply give up because they don't see the progress they expected. Yes, it's heartbreaking when your efforts are not recipro-cated with success, but patience is key. Hustlers under-stand that at the end of the day, it's all about putting as much good quality work out there as possible before something really clicks and fetches success for you. Be patient with yourself; you deserve it.

Another aspect I see is far too common, at least much more common than I'd like it to be, which is the pres-sure of financial planning that people labor under. Retirement planning, in particular, is considered a terrible, terrible burden that needs to be carried on their back every day of their life. I understand that retirement planning is an anxiety-provoking process for many of us. It reminds us that we are entering a phase of our lives where we might not be in control physically, financially, socially, and so on. But the way I look at it is that planning for retirement is the input, and that is all that you can control anyway. The output, which is, of course, the natural function of the input, will be either this ominous feeling of a forced loss of control *or* a much more adaptable perception of relinquishing that control on your own terms. If you have lived your pre-retirement life in a financially prudent manner, focusing on all-around wellness, you can be certain that your post-retirement life will be a fulfilling experience. Sure, there will always be uncertainty, but that's just life, isn't it?

Lastly, the most common mistake that people make when planning for retirement is to think that it's a purely financial decision. Of course, we wouldn't be here having this conversation if money wasn't a crucial factor, but it certainly isn't the only one. Understand that retirement is a major psychological transition too. And as we pointed out before, delaying your retirement would indeed do you more good than retiring early and then simply idling away your time. Remember that the luxury of free time that most hope for in their retirement phase has a decreasing marginal utility—the more you have it, the less appealing it may feel. So my heartfelt plea to you is to live your life; don't trudge through it. Enjoy the journey rather than be overwhelmed by it.

RETIREMENT OPTIMIZATION CHECKLIST

- Generate more income with a side hustle. Be objective in choosing that side hustle—find something that makes you money and also something that you can connect to.
- Rebalance your portfolio at least annually to make sure you are within the age-appropriate risk and reward range.
- Ensure that retirement accounts are not the only place you save for retirement because they tend to have a fairly low limit on how much you can put in there. Get a taxable savings account as well.
- Start looking at retirement not just as freedom from your job but as an opportunity to do a lot more. Plan for creative and enjoyable ways to stay physically as well as psychologically active during your retirement.

5

PREPPING FOR THE BIG DAY

Failing to prepare is preparing to fail.

— JOHN WOODEN

I know what you are thinking: the proverbial "big day" is so far in the future that it's almost impossible to visualize it. Thinking that one day you will be employed and the next day you will not is rather a difficult pill to swallow, without a doubt. But the loss of full-time employment is just one thing that changes. Of course, we have already talked about how you can create steady income streams through annuities, treasury bonds, and stocks. We've also discussed the 4%

rule that applies to withdrawals in retirement. Technically, we have learned a lot about making retirement a little more comfortable!

But no matter how much we try to make our investments and savings match up to our pre-retirement income, it's just not the same, is it? Well, the truth is, your retirement can be exactly as anxiety-provoking or as exciting as you make it to be. You have, of course, been planning the investments and the savings for this phase for a long time now. But now it's time to think about actually living through it.

THE LONG AND SHORT OF MORTGAGE

We spoke earlier of real estate and the value it holds as an investment, but the real estate that holds a very different kind of value for you is surely your home. The sentimental value of your home and the property that it stands on is certainly unmatched. And as you move into your retirement, it wouldn't be unfair to expect that you would have already paid off your mortgage. Traditionally, this has always been the advice that we have received. But it would be prudent to note here that some financial experts in modern times advise that you carry your mortgage into retirement. The idea is to take a loan on your home equity, invest it, and have yet another steady stream of income throughout your retirement. Beware, though—this isn't blanket advice covering all retirees. I won't go into the particular pros and cons of it because I don't recommend it to my clients. I, on the contrary, urge them to think of how amazing it would feel to kiss what's likely your biggest expense, the final goodbye. Call me old-school, but I think paying it off has a lot more merit (both financial and psychological) than dragging it into your retirement.

A 30-year mortgage is a plan that most people seem to prefer. But I strongly recommend that you not take this as the default setting. Explore other options too. I have seen people adopt the myopic vision whereby they are only looking at the immediate payments they will have to make at the end of the month. Since longer mortgages give them smaller monthly payments, they are quick to take them on. What they don't realize is that in this bargain, they are losing thousands of dollars in interest, sometimes even as much as $150,000 or more.

Paying off your mortgage is a triumphant feeling indeed. It instills a certain pride and peculiar confidence in the individual. And besides the interest payments over the years, the pride of total ownership is indeed one of the reasons why I advise people to go with a 15-year mortgage rather than the long-drawn option.

Imagine what paying off your mortgage early would do for you. First and foremost, it frees up a significant chunk of your finances to pursue whatever other adventures you want to take on—travel, setting up a business, investing in new skills that excite you, paying off other debt, and so on. Essentially, that extra wad of cash can open a world of endless possibilities for you. If you can ensure that this added money is invested in avenues that increase your overall net worth—or even sharpen your skill set—that can lead to a greater net worth indirectly rather than in consumables, it can be an excellent boost for your retirement savings.

I want you to take a moment right now to close your eyes and visualize the day when you have paid off your mortgage. Let that moment sink into every fiber of your being. How do you feel at this moment? Enjoy that feeling. Visualize what you are doing now that you have the extra money available. What is it that you want to do? It's this vision that can be your motivation to cope with the tighter finances during a shorter mortgage and enjoy the freedom once it's paid off.

DOWNSIZING YOUR RETIREMENT

Most of us have begun our foray into the independent adult world from the cramped space of our poorly located (and sometimes even weird-smelling) studio apartments. We have all been there. But we all know that life changes. It takes you through all possible adventures, the highlights of which may be climbing the ladder in your career, falling in love, raising a family, and so much more. I am not trying to paint a rosy picture here, but despite the setbacks that we may have had here and there, it's likely that we have upgraded from that cracker-box of an apartment and moved up to maybe moving into your own home where your family grows and blooms within those familiar walls. But imagine this: you are moving towards your retirement, your kids are all grown up and moved out, and now you and your partner are left with this big empty house full of memories. As much emotional value as it holds and as much as it may be something you want to hold onto, is it something you really need or can even afford with your decreased retirement income?

You may argue that if the mortgage is already paid, what difference does it really make? Well, the truth is, a mortgage isn't the only expense that a property incurs. Bigger properties also incur significant maintenance costs, and those are usually the ones that can be the biggest unnecessary drains on your retirement funds. Thus, letting go of your family home in the interest of downsizing during retirement is a legit financial decision that you might have to make. It's not an easy one for sure, especially considering the emotional attachment to it, but it's one that you may consider nonetheless.

Downsizing is nothing but moving out of your big home into a smaller home that is cheaper and fulfills all your retirement needs without excessive expenditures. If you live on the expensive side of town, you might even consider moving to a cheaper neighborhood. By cheaper, I do not mean any less safe—just a place decent enough for you to live a comfortable lifestyle. This is especially true if you have already planned that you want to travel for the most part, or are concerned about the health bills you'll incur, or other special circumstances that you might be expecting.

ESTATE PLANNING

One thing that makes retirement unpleasant for most people is the looming fear of death. It's logical, isn't it? It's against the very nature of our species to surrender to the possibility of an ending; we try until we just can't. The distress springing from this is so high that many people tend to ignore even the legal aspects of this matter. Of course, there's also the tendency to feel like, "Oh, but that's not going to happen to me anytime soon!" Again, while I pray and hope that you remain in the pink of health for a long, long time to come, I must also be the one to remind you to put your legal affairs in place well ahead of time. I have personally witnessed the legal and financial messes that people leave behind, and that's just not something that you would want your loved ones to deal with in addition to loss and grief.

Estate planning is the process of chalking out the what, how, where, and when of the management of your assets in the event of death or even incapacitation in some form. This may involve the transfer of those assets from one generation to the next and the settlement of the taxes the estate may have incurred. Three major tasks that you need to consider are your will, power of attorney, and the setting up of trusts.

Writing Up the Will

A will is a legal document that allows for the unhindered distribution of all your assets after your death to the people of your choice. It would also be the legal roadmap for caring for your minor children if any. This may seem excessively simple on paper, but just because you have created a will, your heirs and loved ones will not be spared the pain of sorting through legal issues related to your passing completely. But the scope of a will is such that it covers most of the essential matters, if not all.

A will, or last will and testament, as it is formally known, generally covers assets like your prized possessions, bank balances, and real estate. It also appoints an executor to execute these instructions after the testator's death. Of course, all of this happens under the supervision of a special court that deals specifically with the issues of wills, known as the probate court. In the absence of a will, it's this same court that will take stock of all your possessions, and depending on the laws, which may be different for different states, these possessions are then divided among the spouse and the children left behind. Other assets, like the life insurance policy or qualified retirement plan, are generally not dealt with by a will as they already have a designated beneficiary that receives these assets directly.

Will's come in many different forms, primarily a standard typed will, a holographic or handwritten will, a joint will signed by two people, a mutual will consisting of two separate wills but largely consisting of similar content, and a pour-over will be used in conjunction with the creation of a trust. Each of these may have different eligibility conditions, but the one common condition is that the signatory is in a sound mental state. Most commonly, people take the route of utilizing the services of a legal attorney to write up their wills, but this is not a mandatory criterion.

Creating Trusts

A trust is an arrangement that helps a trustor channel their assets to a trustee of their choice. The trust is managed as per the terms and conditions agreed upon, and the trustee is handed the responsibility of managing and distributing the assets to the trustor's designated beneficiaries.

Wills are put into motion only after the individual's death. However, a trust can be formed even while the trustor is living and well. This type of trust, which simply requires that assets be transferred to it in order to become active, is known as a living trust. Living trusts may be revocable or irrevocable. In the case of revocable living trusts, the trustor themselves can be named as the trustee and can make changes to the terms of the trust anytime they wish. They can even terminate the trust if they so wish. However, this means that these trusts are still liable for estate taxes. Irrevocable trusts, on the other hand, require the trustor to choose a trustee to manage the trust, over which the trustor now has no control.

On the other hand, if the trust is to be established after the trustor's death, then it would be called a testamentary trust. This would be done via the instructions in a will created prior to the testator's death. The biggest advantage of a trust over a will is that they are not probate-directed, which may decrease the hassle significantly. Also, trusts can surpass the capital gains tax limitations if properly implemented. Since taxes are triggered by ownership of assets, a transfer of assets might succeed in avoiding taxes altogether while still maintaining control.

There are several types of trusts too that can help in special circumstances. Without going into extensive details about each, let's take a quick look at some of the types that might be relevant to you:

1. Qualified personal residence trust: This removes the person's home from their taxable estate so as to reduce the gift tax incurred when transferring assets and can be particularly useful if you expect the property to appreciate in the future.

2. Qualified terminable interest property trust: This ensures that the spouse is taken care of by transferring the assets to the spouse, after whose death the remainder would be divided amongst the children.

3. Charitable trust: This may help lower the incurred taxes as it channels assets to a charity. It may also be arranged as a charitable remainder trust whereby the funds are directed

to beneficiaries for only a certain time period, donating the rest to charity.

4. Separate share trust: Here, a parent may create a trust with different terms and features for each of their children.

5. Blind trust: In this case, neither the trustor nor the beneficiaries have control over or knowledge of how the trustee decided to manage the assets in the trust. This is done to avoid any conflict of interest.

6. Special needs trust: If you have a dependent who's a recipient of Social Security disability benefits from the government, this trust would help them receive income without affecting their benefits.

7. Credit-shelter trust: This allows the assets to grow tax-free, even if they appreciate and grow. It allows the trustor to pass on funds equivalent to the estate tax exemption amount to beneficiaries, while the remaining funds pass on to the surviving spouse tax-free.

8. Generation-skipping trust: These are particularly useful to pass on the assets tax-free to the grandchildren of the trustor.

9. Insurance trust: This removes the life insurance policy from the taxable estate, and the income derived from it is usually used to settle the

estate costs after the trustor's death. However, note that once in this trust, you can no longer change your beneficiaries.

10. Totten trust: Often referred to as the "poor man's trust," it offers the trustor an opportunity to create a trust without any documents or costs. It can be created by using phrases like "payable on death to," "as trustee for," and "in trust for" in the title of the account.

11. Spendthrift trust: This gives protection from the assets being claimed by creditors.

Power of Attorney

It's generally recommended that you designate your power of attorney around the same time as you create your will. This aims at granting a person the power to act on your behalf. In this case, you'd be the principal, and the person you choose would be the attorney-in-fact. This carries a much greater weighting within retirement accounts. This is especially because aging comes with the inherent risk of mental incapacitation in some form. Alzheimer's and dementia, for instance, have been a growing concern among the geriatric population, and it's certainly something that you need to have a contingency plan for.

CHECKLIST FOR RETIREMENT PREPARATION

- Plan for a 15-year mortgage rather than a 30-year mortgage.
- Consider moving to a smaller, cheaper home after retirement.
- Ensure that you have created a will for the management of your assets after your death.
- Make sure you have your power of attorney in place in case of some mishap that compromises your mental wellness.
- Consider creating a trust for the management of your assets even while you are in good health.

SPENDING THE BIG BUCKS

More people should tell their dollars where to go instead of asking where they went.

— ROGER BABSON

The MetLife Employee Benefits Trends Study (2019) suggested that 68% of employees fear outliving their retirement savings. This source of financial stress is only second to concerns about being able to afford healthcare in retirement. That's a pretty high number, wouldn't you say? The root cause of this problem is that most people tend to think of retirement as an event occurring almost in a vacuum. Actually, let's rephrase that; when planning for retirement, most people are interested only in a number, the ballpark figure of *how much* they need to have stashed up before they retire. However, they never pause to consider the contextual contributors to this figure that can render your savings either quite effective or not so much.

Retirement does not take place in a vacuum but in a perpetually dynamic environment with economic, social, psychological, policy-related, medical, and several other factors that create a substantial impact on how much we need to save. The 4% rule of withdrawals that we saw earlier is surely helpful, but it's not written in stone, and it does not work for everyone. Looking at your personal needs in the context of the above-mentioned factors is imperative to creating a retirement plan that clicks into your life as a key clicks into a lock.

By now, we are fairly familiar with the technical details of our retirement plans. Let's take a look at those contextual factors that will impact our spending behavior while in retirement.

THE TAXING REALITY OF TAXES

The fact that your taxes will likely decrease during your retirement is probably not the most exciting or comforting news, simply because the income during retirement is also considerably lower. You have done what you could by saving in tax-deferred or tax-exempt retirement accounts, but that's just half the battle won. Understanding how your retirement income will be taxed is what will get you over the finish line.

Taxes and Social Security

There's often confusion around the taxability of the social security you receive. Well, first off, if that is the only source of income you have in your retirement, there's a big chance you won't get taxed for it by the simple logic that your income will not fall within a taxable bracket. But in addition to this social security, if you do have other income sources, even your tax-exempt interest income, then your social security benefits may become taxable. As people have become increasingly aware of retirement planning, the percentage of households paying taxes on their social security income has clearly increased through the decades. Though that may sting a little, it's not all bad.

Overall, there are three basic steps that go into the calculation of your Social Security taxes.

1. The first step is to calculate your adjusted gross income (AGI). This is determined by the Internal Revenue Service (IRS) by making

certain adjustments to the gross income. These adjustments include deducting expenses like student loan interest payments and certain business expenses. It's based on this income that the IRS arrives at the extent of your tax liability. Generally, the sources that contribute to this income and are considered in this calculation may be your salary, the income from any side gigs that you might take on, the interest and dividends from your investment instruments, and the required minimum distributions from your retirement accounts, and so on.

2. Then the tax-exempt interest is added to the AGI. Remember that this amount isn't liable to be taxed but is still considered in the calculation.

3. This figure is essential for the taxation of your Social Security benefits, as if it's found to exceed the minimum taxable levels, then 50% of your SS benefits are considered taxable. Overall, if your combined income is between $25,000 and $34,000, 50% of your benefits may be taxable, whereas the moment your income jumps beyond $34,000, as much as 85% of your benefits may become taxable. The exact amount of taxes you owe will be based on the tax

brackets determined by the federal government. The IRS gives you all of this information, so go ahead to their website and play around with a few numbers to get an idea of where you stand. If you are not a US resident, then, again, I strongly recommend that you look to your local government for further guidance about how you can make the most of these schemes.

Capital Gains Taxes and Retirement Accounts

We briefly mentioned capital gains taxes before, but now let's get a little deeper into it. Capital gains tax essentially refers to the taxability of the profits earned from the sale of some investment instruments such as stocks, bonds, and mutual funds, as well as real estate and other large-value sales. This tax is due only when the instruments are sold and not when they are merely in your portfolio. These taxes come in two forms: short-term capital gains taxes that are levied on the gains realized by the sale of securities that were purchased within the past year, and long-term capital gains taxes on the profits realized by selling assets that were bought more than a year ago.

The reason they matter to us and our purpose of retirement planning is because retirement accounts help us grow our investments while reducing or avoiding these taxes altogether. So imagine a retirement account with $1 million and growing at 10% every year. If the owner of this account sells all investments and rebalances the replaced investments annually, this fund would grow to almost $1.5 million in the absence of the obligation to pay capital gains taxes. This is why it's crucial to invest in tax-advantaged retirement accounts.

THE FALLING VALUE OF MONEY

The economic variable that will impact your retirement savings and subsequent spending is also the one that you have no control over—inflation. It hits the regular masses where it hurts the most by curbing their buying capacity, which is a function of the rising prices of consumer goods. But that's not all; investors are also strongly impacted by inflation as it's the determining factor in the contribution limits to retirement plans or the fluctuating Social Security. Overall, inflation determines whether the nest egg you are building will really be worth what you are hoping it to be.

According to the LIMRA Secure Retirement Institute, an inflation rate of 1% can take a chunk worth $34,406 out of the Social Security benefits over 20 years, and the amount goes up to a whopping $117,000 if the inflation rate climbs up to 3% (Lake, 2021). Even when inflation rates are low, retirees are the most impacted population, as the expenditures that are of concern to them—healthcare, for instance—continue to be on the rise, regardless of inflation. So, you can be sure that things like healthcare will never be less expensive than they are at present. This can sting more when, due to a low inflation rate, the Social Security Administration (SSA) bypasses bringing cost-of-living adjustment (COLA) into the benefits. COLA is nothing but a rise announced in Social Security benefits and Supplemental Security Income (SSI) to counter inflation.

Even though you may not have any control over inflation per se, understanding inflation patterns may help you calibrate your investments in the most suitable manner possible. Downsizing your home, as we discussed, is one of the ways that you can counteract the effects of inflation. The other option is to focus on investments that will likely increase with rising inflation, like real estate investment trusts (REITs) or even stocks of companies that deal in commodities or services that are likely to become more expensive. While doing this, though, it's of paramount importance that you diversify your portfolio such that there are also more conservative investments that can offer stability in times of uncertainty.

WITHDRAWAL STRATEGIES

I know the aspects we have discussed so far make retirement finances look pretty bleak—taxes and inflation are certainly the most challenging aspects of managing finances post-retirement. But determining how you withdraw from your retirement accounts can offset this in a way that increases your benefits to the maximum. Besides the 4% rule of withdrawal, consider the following strategies to determine how much money you keep at hand for yourself, which largely determines the standard of living you will have.

Fixed-Dollar Withdrawals

This strategy involves withdrawing the same amount of funds every year from your retirement accounts. This is done for a fixed amount of time, let's say five years. This allows you to take home a fixed, predictable annual income and thus helps you optimize your budget accordingly. Due to its simplicity, this strategy allows for quite a manageable financial plan for retirees. Having said that, though, it also comes at the cost of being unable to protect against inflation. This means that the fixed amount that is withdrawn keeps losing its purchasing power with the passing years and may not be able to fulfill your needs. On the other hand, maintaining a higher fixed amount may lead you to run out of your savings sooner. Also, in a relatively down market, you might have to consider liquidating your assets to maintain the amount fixed for withdrawal.

Fixed-Percentage Withdrawals

The other strategy is to withdraw only a certain fixed percentage of your investments every year. This would mean that the exact amount of your withdrawal would depend on the overall value of your portfolio. In this case, a lot is dependent on the percentage you choose to withdraw. If this percentage falls below the expected rate of return on your portfolio, you will actually grow your portfolio by the property of accumulation. Having said that, choosing a percentage that's higher than the expected returns could cause quite a bit of damage to your portfolio by depleting the funds too soon. Also, since the percentage is fixed and not the actual withdrawal amount, it might create a little bit of uncertainty in terms of the annual income.

Systematic Withdrawal Plan

This may seem slightly radical to retirees, as this approach advises the retiree to only withdraw the additional income created by the investments in the portfolio. This may take the form of interest and dividends. This plan, in which the principal amount remains untouched, therefore, allays the fears of running out of retirement savings altogether. Also, since the principal amount is intact, your portfolio will have more opportunities to keep growing. The most significant risk you run is that the additional generated income is proportional to the market performance, which by itself is a fluctuating entity. This plan also doesn't ensure that your withdrawals are keeping pace with inflation.

Withdrawal "Buckets" Strategy

This strategy proposes three buckets or separate accounts holding different assets—the first holding savings in cash, the second holding fixed income securities, and the third holding the rest of investments in equities. These categories are made based on the time remaining until withdrawal and the risk tolerance that the retiree is looking at. These are great to offset the uncertainties within a comparable systematic withdrawal plan. Since short-term and long-term buckets are kept separate, the market fluctuations may impact only the latter. Since they have a long time to go before their withdrawal, the retiree is likely to be less concerned. Though this is a purely psychological impact, it is still enough to keep the investor from making decisions that are driven by panic.

Remember that withdrawals and spending are more than financial phenomena. It also has to do with consumer behavior. Think about it—where are you likely to spend more: in a superstore, where you would have to spend actual cash, or online, where you would put the purchases on a credit card? It's often observed that people spend more in the latter case because somehow it just doesn't *feel* like you are spending as much. The reason it's important to be aware of this because withdrawals and spending cannot always be guided by emotion. Sure, there are some purchases that may hold sentimental value, but your "gut feeling" cannot be the guiding light for your investments and certainly not for withdrawals and spending during retirement. All of these strategies may be useful depending on your personal circumstances, as they provide a solid mathematical understanding of the process and keep the emotions away, at least to a great extent, if not all the time.

7

HACKING RETIREMENT

Age is only a number, a cipher for the records. A man can't retire his experience. He must use it.

— BERNARD BARUCH

You can learn about all the swimming techniques standing beside the pool, but you can bet your life that you will still flounder the first time you take a dip into that water. That doesn't mean that you are dumb or bad at it or any other label you can think of. It just means that sinking is the first step to learning to swim. It's not about learning the techniques or the physics of the whole process. It's only about letting your body acclimatize to the rush of that water, and swimming will eventually happen.

Why is this relevant to your retirement planning, you ask? Well, this is to remind you that no matter how much you learn about the theoretical concepts of savings and investments, you can be certain that you will goof up once in a while, especially when you're just beginning the journey. I am sure while reading all of this, you have probably gone back to the steps you have taken previously in your financial planning and thought, "Why didn't I think of this before?!" The point is not to get too tangled up in the past; just try to put things together from this point forward.

In this chapter, I shall try to answer some of the most common questions that my clients have asked me over the years and also address some of the most common mistakes that they tend to make. This is so that we learn from the missteps and correct them as soon as possible. I avoid responding to these questions straight off the bat because then you might be tempted to treat these answers as quick fixes, which is certainly not the goal here. Remember that these are generalized scenarios that cannot be taken at their face value without context. However, now that we have talked in extensive detail about the context itself, you have earned the right to know about some of the tips and tricks around the retirement planning block.

BRING ON THE QUESTIONS!

I am certain that as you have moved through this book, learning more, you have also probably accumulated more and more questions. But if you understand more, shouldn't that mean that the doubts should vanish? According to Socrates, not necessarily. In fact, he said, "Wisdom is knowing what you don't know." And by those standards, you have only grown wiser. But seriously, retirement plans are not about believing hearsay opinions and assumptions. It's about tailoring your financial circumstances to your needs to the best possible extent. Through this section, we are going to address some of the most common questions that can help clarify things for you.

How do I Go About Planning My Healthcare Costs in Retirement?

You can be sure that healthcare costs are the most unpredictable and likely the biggest expense in retirement. Though, on a subconscious level, our anxieties about losing our health may keep us from thinking about it too much, we must make a conscious attempt to do so. Also, it's crucial that you don't attempt to predict your future health based on where you stand today. Yes, your current health is a significant contributor to how you will generally feel after retirement, but it's certainly not the only one.

People often assume that basic Medicare coverage is all they need to secure themselves from unexpected healthcare costs. This could be quite a costly error. Basic Medicare isn't enough for most. As we saw earlier, the four parts of Medicare—A, B, C, and D— cover very different aspects of healthcare costs. Thus, it would be much wiser to get supplemental coverage like Medigap as well as long-term care insurance. Those belonging to the low-income group may even explore Medicaid if they are pregnant or have children under 18 years of age.

The point is that basic Medicare is rarely enough, and being prepared with backup plans that you may never even use is much better than one hospital stay putting your entire retirement budget into disarray.

I Don't Want to Run Out of Money—How Much Is Enough Really?

As frustrating as it may be, no one right answer exists for that question. And even when you do have a retirement plan, the constantly evolving environment will rarely allow your plan to stay the same as the one you started with. Also, remember that different people like to plan their retirements differently based on their circumstances as well as their own preferences that spring from their personalities. For instance, someone who likes to lay down meticulous plans for the future may start saving much earlier than others. Someone who is likely to play it safe would like to have a considerably more considerable amount stacked away in retirement accounts and otherwise before they even think of retiring.

Our circumstances may or may not always allow us to stick to our preferences, but we may generally arrive at a certain figure by using the 4% rule and our annual spending. Let's say you spend a total of $60,000 every year; then it would be advisable to have at least 25 times that in savings before you retire at, let's say, 65 years of age; so that'd come to $1.5 million. Remember that that figure will increase or decrease if you increase or decrease the retirement age. If you retire later, you might be able to retire with a slightly lesser amount, whereas if you retire earlier, it's recommended that you have at least 30 times what you spend annually.

Saving for retirement is a completely different ballgame than living through retirement with those savings. Whether or not you'll have enough savings to last you through retirement is contingent on how much you spend and earn when in retirement too. If you downsize your lifestyle—and by downsizing, I mean cut the costs that are unnecessary and not the ones that give you joy—and find a paid opportunity to keep you occupied at least part-time, then there's every chance that your savings will prosper along with you.

I Am Still Confused About My Retirement Accounts; what Do I Do?

A common confusion regarding retirement accounts is about the choice of a traditional or Roth IRA. This decision comes down to your expectation of your income and the consequent tax bracket. If you believe that you will have a higher income during your retirement, then a Roth account is the way to go. You might as well pay the taxes now that you are in a lower bracket than later when you expect to be in a higher one. But if you are like most people, it's likely that your retirement income will be lower than your pre-retirement income. In that case, a traditional IRA is your best bet. If you expect to be in the same tax bracket in your retirement as you are now, then I'd recommend a Roth IRA. While the taxes spent would be the same as with a traditional IRA, you would have the advantage of not having to abide by the required minimum distributions (RMDs) after you pass the age of 72 years.

The more confusing is the choice between your own IRA or 401(k). Sure, it doesn't require a genius to know that if your employer offers a matching contribution, then your best path is to invest in your 401(k) at least enough to get the highest matching contribution. But if this is not the case, then is a 401(k) even an option for you? To find the answer to this, you might have to look into options for funds that the plan gives you. A 401(k) is usually a good idea if it allows you to hold low-cost funds. If not, you might be better off setting up your own IRA.

Tell Me More About the Required Minimum Distribution?

RMD has come up in our conversation a couple of times before, and many people are unclear about what this exactly is. It's quite simple, really. Think of it as a safeguard against those who wish to avoid paying taxes altogether. As we mentioned before, tax-deferred accounts let your savings grow without the burden of taxes, and taxes become applicable only when you make withdrawals. You'd think that if you never made any withdrawals, you wouldn't be required to pay any taxes at all. Good plan? Unfortunately, the tax authorities are one step ahead of your scheming to avoid sending money to Uncle Sam. After you reach 72 years of age (prior to 2020, this was 70 years), it's mandatory for

you to withdraw a minimum amount from your retirement accounts, and this is referred to as the required
minimum distribution. If you have multiple accounts,
you may have to consider RMD separately for each
account. Of course, you can take more than the RMD,
which most retirees do.

My Retirement Is Approaching, and I Still Don't Have a Plan! HELP!!

This question is more common than you think, so the
first thing you need to do is take a deep breath and
remind yourself not to panic. Having said that, you
need to get into action immediately. The first step
would be to make the most of your years left in the
workforce. You would find the advice about finding a
side-hustle most useful here. Find something that can
bring in more money, which fulfills a consumer
requirement, and that you can do along with your day
job. You may also want to consider delaying your
retirement age a little so that you can accrue more
earnings than you would have at the conventional
retirement age of 65.

The second step is to organize all your finances. Take a
day off and try to list all the possible sources of income
you have, consolidate the taxes you are paying
currently the sporadic savings that you may have, and
the monthly spending pattern. Once you have these,

you can determine, as discussed above, the amount of money you'd require in savings. This amount might be a much larger amount than you currently have, so do not be overwhelmed by the figure. The idea is not to keep working until you get to that amount but to recalibrate that figure to suit your current situation. This would depend on the maximum amount that you can deposit into savings as well as the maximum income you can rake in. Also, it might be a good idea to delay social security benefits until after your full retirement age is reached.

WHAT NOT TO DO

After I have answered these questions, it generally dawns on people the extent of the mistakes they have been making. Again, the idea is not to ruminate over the mistakes but to see how they can be rectified as soon as possible so as to plug the drains on your finances.

Keeping Retirement Savings For Last

This is the most common mistake I see people make *all the time*. As they believe that they have a long way to go till they retire, they keep prioritizing all other financial needs before retirement planning. For instance, you'll hear people saying (or you might be the one saying it),

"I am going to channel money to my kids' college fund or to my debt fund before retirement—that can wait!" Of course, both of those are super-important; they are just not *more* important than retirement. This is where the envelope system can bring the desired discipline to the fund allocation in your budget.

Early Withdrawals From Retirement Accounts

This is something we have already spoken about, and you mustn't forget that early withdrawals are liable to a 10% penalty. But if you are in absolute need of money, there are a few things you may consider doing before depleting your retirement savings. The IRS permits what are known as hardship withdrawals, wherein you may be allowed to withdraw for immediate and heavy financial needs. These exceptions may include child-birth or adoption expenses, making the down payment on a first home, educational expenditures, and medical costs, especially in the recent past during COVID-19. It's best to consult the IRS website to find the most updated rules in this regard and to see if you qualify for these exceptions. Though you would still be liable for taxes on these amounts, you can certainly avoid paying the penalty.

Overlooking the Intricacies of Social Security

Many assume the federal government's word on Social Security to be the absolute truth and are in no way prone to errors. I hate to burst that bubble for you, but the government can also make mistakes. Therefore, it is advisable to check for these errors and correct them in time to avoid a reduction in your benefits. Your Social Security number gives the Social Security Administration (SSA) access to the record of your earnings and work credits. The SSA mails the Social Security statement to everyone over the age of 25 years at five-year intervals on their 25th, 30th, 35th, 40th, 45th, 50th, 55th, and 60th birthdays. After 60 until retirement, you'll receive these emails every year.

In these statements, you can see an approximate figure depicting the amount of Social Security you might be eligible for after retirement. It's highly recommended that you check whether the social security number on the statement is correct and also whether the earnings listed are accurate. Also, be sure to check the math on the social security calculation itself. If there are any inconsistencies, it's best to get them corrected immediately by either calling the Social Security helpline or making an appointment at your local social security office.

Ignoring Investment Fees

Many people are concerned about the possibility of losing money on risky investments. However, they pay little to no attention to the small amounts of money shaved off of them consistently—even in the safest of investments—in the form of fees. They might not seem like much at the time but can constitute a substantial chunk in the long run. Here are a few tips to keep these fees in check:

- Go for a commission-free online brokerage to trade stocks, mutual funds, exchange-traded funds, etc. There are many available, like Charles Shwab, Robinhood, TD Ameritrade, and so on.
- If you pay monthly maintenance fees for your checking and savings accounts, stop right away and look for free accounts.
- Choose a low-cost HSA from the alternatives available in the market.
- Choose low-cost index funds as discussed previously.
- Look into your mutual funds to see if they are charging you ongoing fees.
- Inspect your 401(k) to see if it incurs any "hidden charges."

- Consider hiring a financial advisor for a flat hourly or session-based fee.

Idling Away the Time in Retirement

The worst mistake you can make in your retirement is to idle away your time. Remember that retirement is as much about relaxing as it is about keeping yourself occupied. Just because you have retired doesn't mean you sit in your lawn chair soaking in the sun and sipping on what's likely sugar-free lemonade on the side. I have personally spoken to numerous people who had this same vision of retirement but got bored of it within the first week. That is when the "holiday mood" ended, and their retirement actually began.

Keep as active as you did before, maybe even more so now that you are free of deadlines and have the time to devote to yourself. I once had a client who was a corporate secretary all her life, but in retirement, she decided to do what she had always loved—cooking and baking. She would bake "keto quiches" thrice every week, and they were an absolute hit at the bakery, where they started selling out within a couple of hours. The bakery begged her to make more, but she took her time giving in to that request. Today, she has a fairly big operation set up, but she paces it to suit her needs rather than bend to the pressures of a boss. That is what retirement is about—not giving up on work but working on your own terms with something that brings you joy.

THE GOLDEN RULES

After learning what not to do, our discussion would be incomplete without talking about what you absolutely *must* do! That's where these rules come in. After gaining a wealth of knowledge about retirement planning, it's quite possible that you are too overwhelmed to begin. Follow these rules to make sure you are on the right track.

Evaluate, Track, and Adapt Your Way to Retirement

From the planning vantage point, the best thing you can do is to keep consistent track of your finances and then come up with some SMART goals. SMART is an acronym that you may have heard of before—specific, measurable, achievable, relevant, and time-bound. Without these criteria, it's impossible to keep track of where you are and where you are headed, especially in financial planning. But the critical thing to remember with these goals is that you might not consistently achieve them in the expected timeframe due to factors outside your control. That does not mean that you scrap them altogether; instead, see how you can best adapt them to your current situation to get you to the desired destination in the end. Keep them as the lighthouse that guides you in the sea of financial uncertainty.

A Diversified Portfolio Can Save Your Life

Diversification doesn't mean that all risk is eliminated. Portfolio diversification helps to mitigate unsystematic market risk by distributing your investments among various instruments that may belong to different asset classes and therefore have different risk profiles, as discussed before. However, systematic market risk is inherent in all investments and can't be eliminated. Most of the time, the unsystematic market risk ends up causing more damage and needs to be protected against. Also, remember that a diversified portfolio may not reap very high rewards as the focus is more on risk mitigation. It may take a while for the investor to find that fine line to balance risk and rewards as per their needs, and so a diversified portfolio is the best, to begin with as a beginner.

There's No Such Thing As the "Right Time to Save" — Start Now

If I had a dollar for every time, someone asked me when the best time to start saving was, I would be so rich that I wouldn't have to save myself! I am just kidding; millionaires and billionaires take their savings much more seriously than we do—maybe that's why they are 'illionaires.' But jokes aside, NOW is the time to save, no matter where you are in your career, how much you earn, or how old you are. No amount of income is ever going to be enough if you are not appropriately focused on savings.

Cash Savings Are NOT the Way to Go

Wads of cash hidden under a loose floorboard are definitely not going to help. If your money is lying dormant, retirement planning will always be an uphill climb. The idea of retirement planning—or any kind of financial planning—is to make your money work for you. Cash does not allow that to happen. So, your $1,000 would remain the same after 10 years, and taking inflation into account; you'd actually be losing money since the money today would have lost value after 10 years. You owe it to yourself to put your money into avenues where it can grow rather than remain stagnant.

Budgets Are Mandatory for a Comfortable Retirement

Budgets are not people's favorites; they are much disliked all across the board by almost all categories of people. But there's no way around them either. Cutting back on things you can, not on things you can't, will help you grow your wealth exponentially when done in a meticulous manner, and you will eventually get to the (almost) perfect retirement that you have always hoped for.

8

THE PERFECT RETIREMENT

Being happy doesn't mean that everything is perfect. It means that you have decided to look beyond the imperfections.

— GERARD WAY

R etirement planning is like preparing for a vision of ourselves that we haven't seen. None of us know if we'll be here to celebrate our 75th birthday, and yet it's imperative that we make this preparation with the utmost seriousness. But understand that your time in retirement isn't only about the money that you save. The scope of your life is much wider than that.

Though up until now, we have been focusing on the financial aspect, we are going to pivot a little from here.

If you remember, I said in the beginning: I don't wish for this to be just another book in the pile of your financial planning books. I want you to be able to push the boundaries of your understanding of the term 'retirement' and see how it's not all about your employment status or finances. The savings can only help you get so far. The rest of the journey is very much dependent on your perception. In this chapter, I would like you to set aside just for a moment the financial details that you have absorbed so far and look at retirement in its entirety.

THE PSYCHOLOGY OF RETIREMENT PLANNING

The way our society is structured, we are conditioned to chase events like jobs, marriages, owning assets, etc., and then build a life around them. You may think since so many of us follow this unsaid notion, it must be true. So, despite being unhappy, you continue to follow in the footsteps of the many before you, chasing rainbows and hoping to someday be so lucky as to find a pot of gold at the end of those rainbows.

Unfortunately, very few discover that pot on this path —not of gold but of fulfillment, which is just as precious. The others keep chasing chimeras until the very end. Turns out, we have got it all wrong—we have been doing the exact opposite of the thing that could lead us to contentment. Turns out the way to happiness is not by building a life around these supposedly important events but by choosing life and then going on to create the events that align with that life. If you have been one to run the rat race, it's time you stop and take a breather. I know I said that financial decisions should not be taken by emotions, but guess what? While that is crucial and 100% true, it's also essential that emotional as well as financial needs are paid attention to when planning for retirement.

Mitch Anthony, the author of *The New Retirementality* (2014), provides an interesting model to determine what your retirement would look like based on what matters to you. He makes use of the famous Maslow's Hierarchy of Needs to propose his own Hierarchy of Financial Needs. Maslow believed that human motivation is based on five tiers of needs. He said that without the fulfillment of the lower tier's needs, it would never be possible to move upwards in the hierarchy. The bottom-most need at the foundation of this hierarchy is survival and physiological needs like food, water, shelter, clothing, and other essentials. On the next rung lie safety and security needs. Next come love and belong-ingness needs; then come prestige and esteem needs; and last comes the need for self-actualization, where a person is on a path towards realizing their full potential.

Anthony has juxtaposed Maslow's model with financial needs to come up with the following model of financial preparation for retirement:

1. Survival income: This is the money you need to have at the bare minimum. Cutting down on all leisure and entertainment expenses, if you kept only those things you needed to survive, what would be the cost incurred?
2. Safety income: This may include the so-called emergency fund that helps us get through uncertain situations in life. It may also include the ability to pay for insurance. Having this income lets, you have at least some peace that there is a backup after all.
3. Freedom income: This is the level of income that helps you explore avenues that lead to your growth—travel, hobbies, education, etc. This inculcates the self-esteem that allows you to flourish.
4. Gift income: At this level, we have income that we can share with our loved ones. The ability to

express gratitude to your partner through a meaningful gift can strengthen the sense of belonging.

5. Dream income: This is an income that will allow an individual to accomplish all the goals they have. Interestingly, it's not so much the amount of income that matters here as much as the path you take to get there.

Pay attention to all of these needs and income levels as they blend into each other. When you think of retirement, what are the needs you envision being fulfilled by what hierarchy of incomes? In a nutshell, think of the money you make and save not just as a way to get through everyday life but as a means to create the life of your dreams.

THE FULFILLMENT CURVE

Working with several clients over the past few decades has failed to give me the answer to a question I have held onto for too long—how much is enough, really? The concept of the Fulfillment Curve is the closest that anything has come to being an answer to that question. Vicki Robin and Joe Dominguez explore this concept in their book *Your Money Or Your Life* (2018). This curve considers the question, "Does money bring happiness?"

Well, the authors propose that in the beginning, money does bring happiness. The first time you started earning and buying yourself the amenities you wanted, maybe eventually even buying an apartment, your own car, and so on, think about how happy it made you. Cut to today. If you buy, let's say, a new car, do you think the joy would compare to what you experienced the first time? Most likely not, and that's precisely what the fulfillment curve purports.

This theory says that there is what can be considered the 'enough' point where a certain amount of money gives you the maximum fulfillment. However, you'd think that the more the money, the more the fulfillment; after this point of 'enough,' things quickly start going downhill, whereby money fails to bring you any additional joy. No matter how much of it you have, you are still not happy. The possessions and the luxuries start to cramp up your space, and it starts feeling more stifling than liberating.

If you haven't found that 'enough' point yet, then now would be a great time because this will be an essential factor in your retirement planning. You get to decide how much is enough, and you get to declutter everything else. Go ahead and explore that point where you feel the money is enough to live a happy life. Remember that as important as money is in retirement, your peace of mind is far more important, and mounds of money are often good at eating away at that peace.

THE BODY, MIND, AND SOUL EXPERIENCE

Erik Erikson, yet another famous psychologist, gave an interesting theory of lifespan development in which he mapped out the various stages that an individual goes through over the span of their lifetime. He speculated on the various psychological tasks and struggles that each stage presents. Those that successfully complete these tasks are relatively better functioning and well adapted. He said in the old age stage, which he called integrity vs. despair, the individual is presented with the task of reviewing their life. Those who look back with a positive outlook and have fewer regrets seem to develop integrity, while those who are focused on all the things they got wrong tend to develop despair. This theory holds a special significance for retirement as it reminds us of the vulnerabilities of retirees. This intense experience of retirees also tells us that retirement is not just a time of financial changes but also a period that introduces changes across all important aspects of their lives.

What you do in your retirement has a massive role to play in whether or not you will develop a regretful stance on your life. So, don't give up on bettering your life just yet. In fact, now is your time! Go crazy with all that you have wanted to do for so long. The idea of old age is heavier than the actual experience of it. Stop telling yourself that you are too old to do something new. That's not to say that you should be recklessly endangering your health and well-being, not at all! If you give it a shot, you might be surprised at how many things there are in this world that you want to do and are in perfect health to do.

When was the last time you did something that brought you pure joy? When was the last time you weren't worried about how other people would react? What would your boss say? What about the children and the neighbors? Well, guess what? You have lived your life based on everyone else's expectations; now, it's time to fulfill some of your own.

It's extremely necessary that you take care of your all-around health and not just the physical aspects. If the idea of retiring feels overwhelming, know that it's natural and you are not alone. Seek help, talk about it, and try to fill your post-retirement life with things that you enjoy. Make a bucket list, if you haven't already— list down all the things you want to do before you die. Whether you get to each one of these or not is secondary, but let the sheer joy of a future filled with possibilities fill you up from within. Extend your social circle and attend classes, which may put you in touch with more like-minded people. Social support has long been shown to boost well-being. So, spend more time with friends and family, and take a fun trip with your loved ones. In short, do everything that helps you care for your physical, emotional, cognitive, social, and spiritual health and any other facet of your life that you can think of.

Know that you deserve all the happiness. And remember that though money is one way to get that happiness, it is certainly not the only way. Go ahead, find your own way to a happy life and a content retirement.

CONCLUSION

There you have it—all that you need to know to begin your retirement planning right away. Be sure to reference more detailed sources on each of the topics we have covered whenever you feel the need to. Before you go on to assimilating the content of this book into your lifestyle, though, I would like you to do a simple exercise.

Sit in a comfortable space with a notepad and a pen where there are no distractions. Close your eyes for a while and try to imagine your life as you wish to see it in your 60s or 70s, or just in retirement in general. Try to visualize all the details that you can think of—the kind of a house you live in if you see yourself with grandkids or pets, or simply hanging out with your friends, or taking a night stroll with your partner, whatever it is that you may wish for yourself. Let the joy of it all soak into your being. Even though actual retirement may be way too far into the future, this joy and this vision will act as the catalyst that boosts your journey to that point.

To solidify this vision, I'd like you to answer a few questions right after you have done this visualization exercise when the feeling of bliss is fresh in your mind and heart:

- How do I picture my retirement? What is my *normal* in that phase of life?
- Is retirement planning important for the vision of retirement that I have? If so, why is it important?
- What changes do I need to make in my life to get to that vision—financially, physically, mentally, or in any other aspect of my life?

Once you have the answers to these questions, you will realize if and how finances weave into your vision for the future. And that's what's much more effective than me giving you all the financial advice you can cram into your head.

My suggestion is that after solidifying this vision in your mind, you decide on a timeline to start putting the different elements of your vision into practice. Do not attempt to do it all at once—you'll only end up over-whelming yourself and giving up in the end. Do it one step at a time. In my experience, 30 days divided into roughly four weeks is a reasonable time period for you to prepare and get into the zone. I usually recommend that my clients break down the mountain of financial planning into manageable hills in the following manner:

Week One: Dedicate this time to planning a budget. Get the intricacies of your cash inflow and outflow accurate down to the tee. Get the envelope system in place.

Week Two: If you haven't yet, get all the details of your 401(k) from your employer. Determine which accounts are the most suitable for you, and get those accounts started as soon as possible.

Week Three: This week, think of growing your wealth by investing in a balanced portfolio—hire a financial advisor for a flat fee to get you started if you feel the need. Also, explore other avenues and hustles that might help you earn some extra bucks. Assess what works for you.

Week Four: Get your taxes in order. This might also be an excellent time to get into the nitty-gritty of your estate planning, which may have significant implications for your taxes as well.

With that, you will have your financial plan firm in place; keep oiling this machine with tracking and rebalancing, and you should be good to go. Again, while doing all of this, remember to automate your finances so that even when you are not watching your money like a hawk, it still keeps flowing in and growing smoothly.

If you have enjoyed reading this book and found it helpful, do consider leaving a review online—it'll surely help me reach many more people that often find themselves struggling the moment financial planning comes up, especially in the context of retirement. As for you, I hope that you remember the squirrel analogy we used right at the beginning of this book because this is really what it all comes down to. Now that we have learned how to gather all the nuts without going nuts ourselves, I hope that you learn how to enjoy them too!

REFERENCES

Anthony, C. (2021 20). *How capital gains tax works on pension funds*. Investopedia. https://www.investopedia. com/articles/markets-economy/083116/how-capital-gains-tax-works-pension-funds.asp#:~:

Anthony, M. (2014). *The new retirementality: Planning your life and living your dreams ... at any age you want.* John Wiley And Sons, Inc.

Ashurst, L. (2009). *Talking about retirement, the secrets of successful retirement planning.* London Kogan Page.

Barney, L. (2016, August 25). *The biggest retirement fear is inadequate savings* | Plan sponsor. Www. plansponsor.com https://www.plansponsor.com/biggest-retirement-fear-is-inadequate-savings/

Beattie, A. (2019). *5 simple ways to invest in real estate.* Investopedia. https://www.investopedia.com/investing/simple-ways-invest-real-estate/

Brainy Quote. (n.d.-a). *Bernard Baruch quotes.* BrainyQuote. https://www.brainyquote.com/quotes/bernard_baruch_130799#:~:text=Bernard%20Baruch%20Quotes&text=Age%20is%20only%20a%20number%2C%20a%20cipher%20for%20the%20records

Brainy Quote. (n.d.-b). *George Bernard Shaw quotes.* BrainyQuote. Retrieved May 23, 2022, from https://www.brainyquote.com/quotes/george_bernard_shaw_161702#:~:text=George%20Bernard%20Shaw%20Quotes&text=Give%20a%20man%20health%20and%20a%20course%20to%20steer%2C%20and

Brainy Quote. (n.d.-c). *George Foreman quotes.* Brainy-Quote. Retrieved May 23, 2022, from https://www.brainyquote.com/quotes/george_foreman_153405

Brainy Quote. (n.d.-d). *Harry Emerson Fosdick quotes.* BrainyQuote. Retrieved May 23, 2022, from https:// www.brainyquote.com/quotes/ harry_emerson_fosdick_100810#:~:text=Harry% 20Emerson%20Fosdick%20Quotes&text=Don

Davis, G. B. (2021, September 14). *11 ways to eliminate investment fees & reduce costs in your portfolio.* Money Crashers. https://www.moneycrashers.com/eliminate-investment-fees-reduce-costs-portfolio/

Fernando, J. (2020). *Index fund.* Investopedia. https:// www.investopedia.com/terms/i/indexfund.asp

Fernando, J. (2021, October 28). *Bond.* Investopedia. https://www.investopedia.com/terms/b/bond.asp

Goodreads. (n.d.-a). *A quote by Anaïs Nin.* Www.-goodreads.com. Retrieved May 23, 2022, from https:// www.goodreads.com/quotes/348099-good-things-happen-to-those-who-hustle

Goodreads. (n.d.-b). *A quote by Gerard Way.* Www.-goodreads.com. Retrieved May 23, 2022, from https:// www.goodreads.com/quotes/342325-being-happy-doesn-t-mean-that-everything-is-perfect-it-means

Goodreads. (n.d.-c). *A quote by John Wooden*. Www.-goodreads.com. Retrieved May 23, 2022, from https://www.goodreads.com/quotes/62225-failing-to-prepare-is-preparing-to-fail

Hale, J. M., Bijlsma, M. J., & Lorenti, A. (2021). *Does postponing retirement affect cognitive function? A counterfactual experiment to disentangle life course risk factors.* SSM - Population Health, 15, 100855. https://doi.org/10.1016/j.ssmph.2021.100855

Hayes, A. (2021, April 21). *Stock*. Investopedia. https://www.investopedia.com/terms/s/stock.asp

Horton, M. (2022, March 20). *How to avoid paying taxes on social security income*. Investopedia. https://www.investopedia.com/ask/answers/013015/how-can-i-avoid-paying-taxes-my-social-security-income.asp#:~:text=Up%20to%2050%25%20of%20Social

Investopedia. (2022, January 2). *Treasury bonds: A good investment for retirement?* Investopedia. https://www.investopedia.com/ask/answers/041515/treasury-bond-good-investment-retirement.asp

Investopedia Team. (2020). *A real estate investing guide.*

Investopedia. https://www.investopedia.com/
mortgage/real-estate-investing-guide/

Johnson, H. (2021, November 14). *I wiped out my emergency fund years ago, and there are 3 reasons I never plan to
rebuild it.* Business Insider. https://www.
businessinsider.com/personal-finance/reasons-dont-
have-emergency-fund-2021-11?r=US&IR=T

Kagan, J. (2021, July 14). *Last will and testament.* Investopedia. https://www.investopedia.com/terms/l/last-
will-and-testament.asp

Kagan, J. (2022, May 2). *Defined-Benefit plan.* Investopedia.
https://www.investopedia.com/terms/d/
definedbenefitpensionplan.asp#:~:text=A%20defined%
2Dbenefit%20plan%20is

Lake, R. (2021, December 6). *How to plan for medical
expenses in retirement.* Investopedia. https://www.
investopedia.com/retirement/how-plan-medical-
expenses-retirement/

Lioudis, N. (2021, January 29). *The importance of diversification.* Investopedia. https://www.investopedia.com/
investing/importance-diversification/

McFarlane, G. (2021, June 15). *Why emergency funds could be a bad idea.* Investopedia. https://www. investopedia.com/articles/personal-finance/123113/ why-emergency-funds-are-bad-idea.asp

MetLife. (2019). *Thriving in the new work-life world | MetLife's 17th annual US employee benefit trends study 2019.* MetLife.

O'Brien, S. (2019, June 9). *Considering basic Medicare with no backup insurance? That could be a costly mistake, experts say.* CNBC. https://www.cnbc.com/2019/06/ 07/considering-basic-medicare-with-no-backup-insurance-is-a-big-mistake.html

Panico, M. R. (2021, June 23). *To be happy in retirement, don't be afraid to use your "nuts."* Kiplinger. https://www. kiplinger.com/retirement/happy-retirement/603012/ to-be-happy-in-retirement-dont-be-afraid-to-use-your-nuts#:~:text=A%20University%20of% 20California%20at

Patel, N., Vlaskovits, P., & Koffler, J. (2016). *Hustle: The power to charge your life with money, meaning, and momentum.* Vermilion.

Pinkasovitch, A. (2021, December 15). *Retirement savings: Tax-Deferred or tax-exempt?* Investopedia. https://www.investopedia.com/articles/taxes/11/tax-deferred-tax-exempt.asp

Probasco, J. (2022, February 11). *How much money do I need to retire?* Investopedia. https://www.investopedia.com/retirement/how-much-you-should-have-saved-age/#:~:text=Most%20experts%20say%20your%20retirement

Quote Fancy. (n.d.-a). *Roger Babson quote: "More people should learn to tell their dollars where to go instead of asking them where they went."* Quotefancy.com. Retrieved May 23, 2022, from https://quotefancy.com/quote/1076855/Roger-Babson-More-people-should-learn-to-tell-their-dollars-where-to-go-instead-of-asking#:~:text=Roger%20Babson%20Quote%3A%20%E2%80%9CMore%20people

Quote Fancy. (n.d.-b). *Tom Ford quote: "There are no right or wrong answers; there is only intuition."* Quotefancy.com. Retrieved May 23, 2022, from https://quotefancy.com/quote/1191709/Tom-Ford-There-are-no-right-or-wrong-answers-There-is-only-intuition

Rao, J. (2011, January 19). *Ten golden rules for retirement planning*. CNBC. https://www.cnbc.com/2011/01/19/ten-golden-rules-for-retirement-planning.html

Robin, V., Dominguez, J. R., & Tilford, M. (2008). *Your money or your life: 9 steps to transforming your relationship with money and achieving financial independence*. Penguin Books.

Sato, G. (2022, January 12). *How to make a retirement budget*. Www.experian.com. https://www.experian.com/blogs/ask-experian/how-to-make-retirement-budget/

Schwahn, L., & McMullen, L. (2021, February 4). *Goodbudget review: A hands-on digital envelope system*. NerdWallet. https://www.nerdwallet.com/article/finance/goodbudget-app-review

Simon, J. (2022, January 7). *How to calculate the required minimum distribution (RMD)*. SmartAsset. https://smartasset.com/retirement/how-to-calculate-rmd

Smith, L. (2021). *What is a will, and why do I need one now?* Investopedia. https://www.investopedia.com/articles/pf/08/what-is-a-will.asp

Warren, E., & Warren Tyagi, A. (2006). *All your worth: The ultimate lifetime money plan*. Free Press, ©B.

Whiteside, E. (2019). *What is the 50/20/30 budget rule?* Investopedia. https://www.investopedia.com/ask/answers/022916/what-502030-budget-rule.asp

Made in the USA
Coppell, TX
24 January 2023

11654003R00094